FLOWERS IN THE MINEFIELDS

El Alamein to St Honorine

FLOWERS IN THE MINEFIELDS

El Alamein to St Honorine

JOHN JARMAIN - WAR POET

1 9 1 1 - 1 9 4 4

— • —

A short appraisal of his life and work by

JAMES CROWDEN

Essays by Joe Dean and John Kaestlin

FLAGON
PRESS

Published in 2012 by Flagon Press
Forge House, Fore Street, Winsham, Chard, Somerset TA20 4DY
www.james-crowden.co.uk

Poems © Estate of John Jarmain 1945
Poems first published by Collins 1945
A limited edition of war poems published by Hawthorn Press 1995
Poems have also appeared in Salamander Oasis Trust anthologies

Original foreword © John Kaestlin 1945
Short Essay on John Jarmain by Joe Dean © Joseph Dean 1948
Introduction – John Jarmain – In the Front Line © James Crowden 2012
A few brief historical comments © James Crowden 2012

Photographs reproduced by kind permission of the Imperial War Museum.
See individual image credits. All Jarmain photographs and letters courtesy
of Janet Coward. The photograph of John Jarmain and BSM John
MacPherson on the opposite page courtesy of John MacPherson, Oban.
Map of 51st Highland Division start line at El Alamein reproduced by kind
permission of The National Archives, Kew, ref. WO169/4292

ISBN: 978-0-9562778-3-1

British Library and Cataloguing-in-Production Data
A catalogue record for this book is available from the British Library

Design by Andrew Crane
Typeset in Lapidary 333
Printed and bound by the Short Run Press Limited, Exeter

*'And the desert will live in us
when war is ended'*

CAPT JOHN JARMAIN
AND BATTERY SGT MAJ JOHN MACPHERSON
OUTSIDE BATTERY HEADQUARTERS, QASSASIN,
EGYPT, AUGUST 1942
NOTE THE PORTABLE AIR RAID SIREN.

ACKNOWLEDGEMENTS

Preparing and researching this book has taken me into some marvellous backwaters. First of all I must thank Christopher Richards for alerting me to John Jarmain's existence in the first place and his connections to Somerset. Then to Professor Tim Kendall of Exeter University for putting me in touch with John Jarmain's daughter, Janet Coward as well as the various meetings we had in River Cottage Canteen in Axminster discussing the project. To Dawn Bellamy for letting me look at excerpts from her PhD thesis on 2nd World War Poets which included comparisons between John Jarmain and Keith Douglas. To Prof. Jon Stallworthy of Wolfson College, Oxford, for his advice, time, good counsel and encouragement.

I am very grateful to Janet and Dick Coward who have helped me to source poems, photographs, letters and Jarmain family history. To Felicity Cox for typing the letters up in the first place. To Joanna Weston in Canada for allowing me to use the sketch of John Jarmain made by her mother, Eve Houghton.

To Jenny de Gex for research in the Pilton area. To Carol Penman in Australia for her help in remembering the early days of Jarmain's life in Somerset. To Dick Shilton the archivist at Millfield School. To Len Barnett for his research at the National Archives at Kew in ferreting out various war diaries for 61st Anti-Tank Regt Royal artillery and 51st Highland Division. To John MacPherson of the Oban War and Peace Museum for various photographs. His father, also called John MacPherson, was Battery Sergeant Major for 242 Battery. Thanks to Aulay Dunn also of Oban, for the memories of his father, Major Harry Dunn who commanded the battery during the war. Thanks in particular to Sergeant Harry Garrett for sharing his vivid memories of El Alamein and the fighting in North Africa.

To Paul Evans at the Royal Artillery Library, Woolwich for his help on certain technical matters to do with anti-tank guns. To Dr. Diana Henderson and Dr. Jonathan Holmes of Queens' College Cambridge. To Cairistiona NicCoinnich (Christine Mackenzie) Secretary Urras Shomhairle (The Sorley MacLean Trust) c/o Sabhal Mòr Ostaig, Isle of Skye. Ian Livingstone of the 51st Highland Division - Online Museum.

Flagon Press is very grateful to Eland Books for permission to use the quote from 'Libyan Sands' by Ralph Bagnold. Eland Books act on behalf of the Ralph Bagnold's estate. 'Libyan Sands', an excellent book, which is still in print Eland Books 2010 see **www.travelbooks.co.uk**. Flagon Press is grateful to Curtis Brown for permission to use the quote by Vita Sackville-West. Angus MacIntyre webmaster of **www.salamanderoasis.org**. To The Times Literary Supplement / NI Syndication for permission to use the TLS review quote written by Alec M Hardie. To The Imperial War Museum for allowing me to reproduce their photographs. I am very grateful to the Society of Authors for helping to clarify copyright issues.

In particular I am very grateful to Ptolemy Dean and his family for allowing me to reproduce his father's fine essay on John Jarmain. And in the same vein, I am very grateful to Dr Jürg Kaestlin of Zurich for allowing me to reproduce the excellent foreword written by John Kaestlin to the original edition of the Jarmain poems.

Thanks are also due to Catherine Simmonds who helped in the early stages of the book and to Penny Dunscombe who proof read and copy edited much of the material. To Andrew Crane who very patiently designed the book and to Short Run Press in Exeter who printed the book.

James Crowden

JOHN JARMAIN
FROM A SKETCH BY EVE HOUGHTON

FLOWERS AND MINEFIELDS

The title of this book *Flowers in the Minefields* is drawn from a line of John Jarmain's poem 'El Alamein', and can be taken to refer not just to the actual flowers, the asphodel lilies that come out in spring, but to the anti-personnel mines which were laid by the Germans in the Devil's Gardens. In many senses the 'flowers' are also the poems which have grown out of the warfare in the western desert.

Interestingly the asphodel lilies, to which Jarmain is referring, also have a direct connection with Greek mythology. The 'asphodel meadows' are where the souls of people who lived lives of near equal good and evil rested, on a neutral plateau - obviously a few notches down from the Elysium Fields. These asphodel flowers were the favourite food of the Greek dead. The meadows are described as a ghostly place. Homer describes the plant as being deeply connected with the underworld. Asphodel lilies are often planted on graves and its link with death is due no doubt to the greyish colour of the plant's leaves and its yellowish flowers, which suggest not only the gloom of the underworld but the pallor of death itself. Persephone, the goddess of vegetation, often appears with a garland of asphodels. So it is fitting that the battlefield of El Alamein which saw so much death should be thus adorned.

Here is an extract from a few lines of Jarmain's taken from his sonnet 'Failure' written in February 1944.

> *"By fate opposed*
> *Men prove their purpose, in the dangerous hour*
> *Their brief excelling brilliance is disclosed;*
> *When threatened most the soul puts forth its flower."*

CONTENTS

THINKING OF WAR

If I must die, forget these hands of mine
That touched your body into tiny flames:
Forget our faith, our strength, and each least sign
— The whispered wonder of our own two names
And all great words we said: how love was true
And seemed immortal. O, forget, my love,
That there was one on earth who worshipped you
And only for your sake desired to live.

I shall forget. As if I never lived
Will be the hours we had, the years we missed,
And your grief too. These hands that have so loved
Will be dumb then as hands you never kissed,
And all my body will not know your name.
I shall have broken our faith: do you the same.

JUNE 1939

6-POUNDER ANTI-TANK GUN CALLED 'RASTUS'
3 NOVEMBER 1942
© IMPERIAL WAR MUSEUMS (E 18895)

This desert army is unique, it has a character all its own. My division has a sufficiently pronounced character, you would think, but this desert army has a character more definite even than that, and deeper-rooted because it is based on something bigger and more enduring than itself — on the desert.

JOHN JARMAIN

We were a little afraid of the western desert, not so much because it was waterless and entirely uninhabited but because it was different from all experience...

The western desert has also always been a land of mystery.
There are deserts and deserts....

RALPH BAGNOLD – *LIBYAN SANDS*, 1935

We lived outside the world, beyond the borders Of the lands men use.

JOHN JARMAIN OUTSIDE HIS DOOVER WITH 'GOD' AND THE DESERT, NEAR EL AGHEILA

SHORT ESSAY ON JOHN JARMAIN
BY JOE DEAN

I remember a March morning on the Banffshire coast four years ago. I was a Second lieutenant in a Highland anti-tank Battery. The Battery Captain, whom I had not met, came to lunch. He was living away in the Spey Valley, commanding the Divisional School of Bombs and Mines. He lunched in our Mess, which was in the pub on the street corner going steeply down to the fishing port. He did not look like a soldier, like the traditional soldier. He had thick wrinkled black hair behind a domed forehead, almost Shakespearian: a long thin nose, thin lips, thin fingers, sensitive, humorous, a laugh that seemed to come from a hilltop, the figure of a runner, not a wrestler. He neither talked nor walked like the soldier of tradition, but with conscious enjoyment and with conscious grace. It turned out that he was nothing of a Sapper, though our expert in explosives. He was not a Scotsman, though in the Highland Division. Though attached to Divisional Headquarters, he was least of all a Staff Officer. These are commonplace incongruities in the Army: we grow used to them, and bear them without surprise. But plainly he had not grown used to them, and he valued surprises. He attached importance to all manner of things, and especially to words. He emphasized with laughter the unlikelihoods and impossibilities. He savoured the incongruities:

The ants, the shreds of my hair, the buried city
(Passed and a fable now, the glory of the Lepticans),
They are all disconnected, irrelevant one to another,
Incongruous. So I found them; so I have set them down.

This was my first meeting with John Jarmain, who may be remembered as one of the poets of this last war. A month later, he rejoined the Battery in Aldershot, whence

In undetected trains we left our land
At evening secretly, from wayside stations,

and for two years travelled, following the zigzag of strategy, with our guns. I saw a lot of him: in ships, in battles, in dug-outs, in dust and in the dawn and in the night, in cities. As he wrote of his poems, so I feel of my memories:

You who in evenings by the fire
May read these words of mine,
How let you see the desert bare
In the print-smooth line?

They had no peace at their creation,
No twilight hush of wings;
Only the tremble of bombs, the guns' commotion,
And destructive things

First impressions soon deepened. All the time he balanced his passionate enjoyment of things with reticence, almost with silence. I remember an evening during the battle of Mareth when by the light of his paraffin lamp he was struggling with a poem on the battle of Alamein: he agreed, he said, with Matthew Arnold that poetry came from emotion recollected in tranquillity. He tried for a balance, not by subtraction from the weighted arm of the scale, but by addition to the other – a balance of full measure. Yet he hated unnatural excess of the body as much as the easy natural surrender of the mind. By continued effort of all faculties he kept his focus sharp. He knew that character was created by will:

> *It is not death nor destiny nor age*
> *Nor any such superb antagonist*
> *That works the soul's defeat,*

but

> *Day by day*
> *The precious hours like vacant windows passed,*
> *The pretty vision and the soft delay,*
> *These bring defeat and rust the sword we bear,*
> *Diminish each bright purpose; till at last*
> *All's wasted, and the heart's too dull to care.*

He did not know this personal failure. Nor did he know the recognition of his writing, after he was killed in Normandy. The following month, his first novel, *Priddy Barrows*, written before the war, was published, and at the end of 1945 the thin collection of his poems was brought out, and is most deservedly still in print. The poems, none of them long, are arranged pyramidically: first, poems in war-time, the last two written in the waiting time between return from the Mediterranean and D-Day, and then poems in peace-time leading back to his early youth. The quotations in this article are taken from this volume.

But he knew success as a soldier. He commanded a new Battery, which was created Eve-like from the ribs of the Regiment, and was the pride of some 150 men before it was disbanded, when all was over, on the Westphalian plain. In command he was clear and warm – a rare mixture, and this success seemed to give an outer frame to the balance he had made within himself. I saw him last in a Dressing Station in Normandy, for a few words, before I was despatched to hospital in England. We were being forced to withdraw from the village of St. Honorine. The situation was not at all clear, but three of my four guns were in the village. I asked him to get them out. It was a mad, not to say unconscionable, request. He said he would try. What happened, I learnt long afterwards. We withdrew entirely from the village, on orders from above, and the enemy occupied it. That afternoon John Jarmain, against all persuasion (we had always more guns to spare than gunners and gunner officers) returned and brought out the guns, without a scratch on paint or person, and also my Jeep with its wireless, even with my beret where I had left it on the seat. He was congratulated by the CRA. The beret I shall always treasure as a memento of such friendship. It was some days later that he was killed in the same village.

J. J. Dean.

FROM 'MODERN READING 17'
EDITED BY REGINALD MOORE. 1948

ORIGINAL INTRODUCTION
BY JOHN KAESTLIN

Taken from a letter written by Captain John Kaestlin,
Jarmain's second in command in Sicily & Normandy

"John Jarmain served throughout with the 51st Highland
Division, as you know; he was with them in Scotland, went
abroad with them, fought with them from Alamein to
Caen, as an anti-tank gunner. I personally saw little of him
during the African campaign as he was then a captain in a
different battery; once at Tripoli, the night before we
moved up to the frontier; occasionally at the various wadis
of Mareth. I didn't really get to know him till after it was
all over and we were training for combined operations in
Algeria. He came over to command a battery I had helped
form at Enfidaville. That was May 8, '43. But from then
on we were constantly together, I as his second in
command, throughout Sicily and – however briefly –
France, sharing our duties and much of our leisure.

"He was killed early on June 26, 1944, in Ste
Honorine la Chardonnerette, a small village which
formerly had the reputation of being the most beautiful in
Calvados but which now, like so much of that desolate
plain, remains an amorphous welter of stony substances.
At the time it was the most advanced point in our line east
of Caen and of the Orne.

"The evening before he had sat late in my doover at
Ranville. First he wrote a couple of letters, one to his wife,
one to the wife of a sergeant we had buried the night
before. Then, amid a series of perhaps more expressive

silences, we just talked, as we had talked away so many evenings before, of Cambridge, friends, books, things in general, the battery in particular. He was, I thought at the time, in a remarkably good mood: unusually excited even, about the morrow and a big attack due to come off which – thoroughly browned off as we were with multiple mortars and trees and being cooped up in our bridgehead – inevitably promised to be the long-expected break-out and Paris 'swan'. We speculated about that. Then, finally, as if again by way of premonition, we went through the whole battery together, man by man, considering personalities and abilities, promotions, desirable changes.

"He had, earlier, been toying with the idea of going down to Honorine at dawn to visit the troops in position there. Normally we took our early morning rounds in turn; but he had had little sleep of late and was completely worn out, eyes bloodshot with dust and fatigue. I wanted him to have a late morning; he certainly needed it. I could so easily have gone. Besides the village was not directly involved. But he wouldn't hear of it and became increasingly adamant under persuasion. Dawn was likely to be pretty sticky down there and he wanted to be with his men when things happened, if they did. So there was nothing to it but a weak compromise: he'd go straight to bed on getting back and leave the rest of the day to me – which wasn't in character anyway. He left me past midnight; but an hour later, returning from seeing some vehicles back into the area, his pipe was still glowing by the mouth of his doover and I gave him the O.K.

"I was awakened at 5 next morning by his batman in a state of obvious agitation. The major had been hurt; he thought seriously. They had left together at 4 o'clock in his jeep. All was perfectly quiet as they drove over the crest and down the long incline to Honorine; but, as luck would have it, on arrival at the village they found the tanks still moving out into position. The noise had attracted the Hun and a mortar concentration had come over as they reached and were held up at the cross-roads. Jarmain, walking, had dived for a slit-trench by the roadside. He never got there. His driver-batman, untouched though necessarily tied to the wheel, found his body in the half-light when it was all over and carried him to the near-by aid post. That done he had driven straight back to tell me.

"I got down to Honorine as fast as I could make it. By now, however, it was fully light and I had to walk most of the way. When I got there he had been dead for some time, and there had evidently been no hope. A piece of shrapnel had entered the base of the skull and he had died, while being evacuated, without regaining consciousness.

"So we buried him, that afternoon, in the 6th Airborne cemetery by Ranville church, a stone's throw from his last headquarters. As many of the battery as could be spared out of the line and a large number of his friends in the division attended. But no one, I think, quite realised what it was all about.

"John's was no ordinary battery. It was, we liked to think, rather unique, at least distinctive. Its character certainly did not long survive him, as it could not have done being largely his. Those of us who were with it from the beginning cannot disassociate the unit from the commander; and in our memories, so graphic and inevitably crystallising in the passing incident, round a series of place names, he is always the central figure. Bougie – the sandy beach of the Algerian bay of that name on which we took shape, first became a separate and real entity. Dreamy Portopallo and the peaceful sunshine of the landing; Vizzini – 'an inverted flowerpot in a saucer' – and the litter of the departed Hun; the angry farmsteads of Ramacca; the topographical perils of the Marine Drive; Sferro – those dusted sun-bleached hills of Southern Sicily from which (for how short a while really) it seemed one would never emerge; not, at anyrate, until suddenly we looked down on the green oasis of Etna. And against all this, and all it revives, John in his jeep, covered in dust, driving unceasingly from troop to troop, to Brigade, to Division, or striding nonchalantly round his guns, his aquiline features and the old red cap he always wore in battle, puffing at his briar, swinging the hazel stick which was, and apparently always had been, his constant companion – always on the spot when things were sticky, encouraging, fathering his men and junior officers through their more trying moments.

"And then the relaxation. The warm still nights high above the Simeto where free from interference from either Hun or mosquito one lay brazenly on the hump of the hill watching the stars and their intriguing shadows below. The view back over the misty yellownesses of the immediate past from the almond orchard of Santa Maria di Licodia on the slopes of Etna; the long dragging climb to the crater; Linguaglossa – the little terraced house on the road through Piedimonte to the sea; Sparta di Messina and all it meant of refound civilisation and culture. Names rich in association which in retrospect are John to an extent that cannot be explained.

"Back in England. The bleak drippingness of it (but it was home and no one was caring). The expectations of spring, and that incredible white elephant that was Dullingham Hall. Suddenly France, and half-forgotten war. Those shell-torn villages of the Orne bridgehead – visions of broken trees and dangling wires, of glass, tame rabbits and dead foals: Ranville, Herouvillette, Escovil, Longueuval and Ste Honorine. And John again, tireless, shepherding as before, fathering. The red hat; the pipe, and the hazel stick...

"To draw the character of one with whom one was so closely associated through so memorable a series of events is an alarming undertaking. Knowledge apart, he was a man of very obvious capacity, combining in no small degree a number of qualities rare in themselves and certainly the rarer in their particularly happy associations and contrasts. I can but signal a salient few. He had, first, a pervasive personality, a blend of the forceful and benign, calm and deliberate and unhesitatingly confident, yet tempered in all things by an innate horror of infringing the mental preserves of another being. That, and its corollary, above all things. Authoritative therefore but never domineering, quiet and reserved but never self-effacive, an eager talker but never dogmatic nor merely a passive listener. Commanding was a duty from which he derived no particular satisfaction save in its execution. Similarly the communal aspect of army life was itself an imposition, if only as a constraint on his choice of contacts. He was too independent to be anything but selective. Just as personal discipline and respect for the essential privacies of feeling and intellect were the lights of his own ethic, he expected them in others – or rather did not expect them but simply avoided the company, outside necessity, of any that offended against that code in speech or manner. He never liked people simply because they liked him. In uncongenial circumstances he was naturally reserved, made no revelations. Among friends, though never expansive, he inspired something of his own collected sense of values and importances, radiated in no small degree that extraordinary inner vitality which was perhaps his most immediate characteristic.

"On analysis that vitality was itself the product of two marked and complementary factors. He had on the one hand an almost preternatural quickness of brain, due partly no doubt to his Huguenot descent on his father's side, partly to his being, academically speaking, a mathematician. At least the taking of a mathematical degree at Cambridge controlled and perfected in its constant application a predisposition to clear and rapid thought. No more than that; no question certainly of the ivory tower, rather the contrary. His was a very sensible, tactile, reality. On his mother's side he acquired his emotional corrective in a vivid awareness and an honest full enjoyment of the countryside. His was a conscious and calculated awareness, the satisfying awareness of Bobi in *Que Ma Joie Remeure*, a book in which he found reflected so much of himself. He had an uncanny way of noticing things, without seeming to, whether it was a yellowhammer in the hedge as he sited a gun or a remark one did not make. Little escaped him. His awareness afforded him the most abiding pleasure; and, again, it was his accurate appreciation of mood and atmosphere, coupled with his intense interest in things around him, which maintained that fresh wide outlook he always had on life, his deep understanding of the natural and the human. As one of his fellow battery commanders remarked the morning he died: 'John was the most human man I ever knew.'

"As to religion frankly he had none in the accepted sense, but was nevertheless no agnostic. Too much of a rationalist equally for blind faiths and blind disbeliefs, and too sufficient to require their artificial support, he denied nothing and was happy believing nothing. He always took every small happiness in both hands and savoured it to the full. He was, in a word, so vividly alive. One cannot, somehow, feel he would enjoy being merely a spirit.

"Add to the above his essential normality, his wide critical reading, his complete honesty of feeling and absence of pretence, his enjoyment of quality in all things and keen eye for the bogus, his unconditional refusal to delegate responsibilities, and finally – but far from least – his absorbing conscientiousness in the job in hand, whatever that might be.

"The job in hand was, of course, commanding a battery, and he gave it his all. Everything else, temporarily, took second place. Had to. He thought a great deal of his battery, and his men, in turn, thought a great deal of him. The affection he inspired, certainly without seeking it, was something out of the way even under conditions in which emotions naturally tend to run abnormally high. His personal example in battle, his profound comprehension of the human and his quickness and sureness of decision inspired a confidence and loyalty throughout the battery, created a moral cohesion, which mere discipline can only provide in palest substitute. His sudden death came as a tremendous shock to all ranks.

"Whether he took risks or no is irrelevant. He did; and on frequent occasions was more than lucky to get away with it. But to do that kind of job properly one has to take risks, accept them; and he would never have slipped up on his responsibilities. His death was so typically John – fitting in a way rather than merely wasteful that he lost his life, not in the thick of a battle in which his decision, locally, could have swayed the issue, but just in visiting his men.

"What else is there of John during that year? He wrote. He had always written – poetry, stories – and continued to do so throughout Africa and Sicily to the extent that time and the Hun allowed. He did not speak about it, maintained a reticence on the subject only too well in keeping with his sense of privacy. It was important to him. He had a noticeable, and at first mystifying habit of secluding himself in his doover of an evening or whenever work was done – which of course was rare during an actual campaign – seemed to like being alone. He would steal the interval, get back as it were to realities, away from the army and war. He would write, or correct some previous draft of which he kept a folder for constant revision, or work at his Italian (which in point of fact he spoke pretty fluently) or relax with one or other of the few books he always had with him: *Alice in Wonderland*, Browning, D'Annunzio, Shakespeare or somebody or other's Book of Birds – for birds and bird-life was perhaps his main outdoor interest apart from just walking.

"To wind up – the final portrait emerging from the above. The aquiline features, gentle and intelligent eyes, the wisp of hair from under the red cap, the ready smile round the inevitable pipe, and the stick. The setting: Africa, Sicily, Normandy. The incidental features: 193 – mathematics – birds – poetry – Italian; *Alice in Wonderland* and D'Annunzio. He was a man of such evident ability who could have achieved so much given the chance. About the chance pointless now to speculate. He was 33. The further tragedy of it was that in fullest maturity his capacities were by force of necessity concentrated on the vital and pleasurable but ultimately ephemeral job of commanding men in battle. Giving of his all to it he had little time for anything else, bar of course being an extraordinarily nice person and excellent companion. His writing, which he took so seriously, was necessarily only a beginning. And so, though what he left he left in final form and to his satisfaction, he would have regarded it. These verses, *Priddy Barrows* and the abiding memory of a few, are all his present. We have all been robbed of his future."

A BRITISH CRUSADER TANK PASSES A BURNING
GERMAN PZKW MK IV TANK DURING OPERATION
CRUSADER (18 NOVEMBER–30 DECEMBER 1941).
JUST ONE OF THE MANY BATTLES THAT PRECEDED
EL ALAMEIN © IMPERIAL WAR MUSEUMS (E 6751)

JOHN JARMAIN – IN THE FRONT LINE
BY JAMES CROWDEN

Men react differently to war. Some become silent, some get drunk, others seek solitude. In the firing line they are often caught between the two worlds of killing and being killed. In the heat of battle fear can trip them up at any moment. Words are difficult to find, because often there are no words to describe what they have just seen or felt or experienced, only orders to 'keep your head down' or 'fix the bayonet' or 'load that gun'. Fear is also apparent in the anticipation of battle and the mental re-enactment afterwards. Painful memories are often repressed and dreams can easily become nightmares.

But words can also have the power to slowly release that fear. They can chart it or mask it. Poetry has the ability to make sense of the dilemmas that soldiers face in the front line and the incongruous nature whereby men are pitched in battle against other men often speaking and thinking in another language, obeying different but similar orders, different rules of grammar and even linguistic logic. Yet in war there is often only one logic: killing.

How the mind manages to survive in such situations is still something of a mystery. There are often delays in psychological and emotional reactions. Horrendous images can be stored up for many years, and yet in the odd moments when there is a lull in the fighting, the mind often reaches out to some familiar image or memory far removed from battle.

Some write letters home, some take photographs as if they were on holiday, some sing to themselves, others write poems if they can; but all the time they are aware of censorship: self-censorship and military censorship. Some censorship is subconscious and falls into predictable patterns, and some is all too conscious. The fact that they can put pen to paper at all is remarkable. They all have to choose their words carefully, so as not to give away their position or any hint of casualties or units on the move or battle plans. The censor's pen, usually their commanding officer's, will go through their letters with sharp rapidity. 'Careless talk costs lives.' In letters, they soon learn to reassure those at home whilst hiding their own inner fears. It is a fine line to tread; and although not ideally suited to war, because of their acute sensitivities and powers of inner observation, poets are unusually adept at walking that particular tightrope. In their poems they can forge their own inner reality, though even these may well be censored.

Born in 1911 in Hatch End, Pinner, William John Fletcher Jarmain was the son of a chartered surveyor. The Jarmains were proud of their Huguenot roots and had done well for themselves as solicitors in London. There was even a firm called Scott, Jarmain, Trass and Jarmain. His mother, Mary, known as Marzi, was the daughter of an auctioneer from Romford, Essex. John did well at school and by the age of thirteen he had gained a scholarship to Shrewsbury School. He must have been well aware of the war poetry written by Wilfred Owen who was also educated in Shrewsbury. At school Jarmain was a bit of a loner, but did well and managed to get a place at Queens'

College Cambridge to read Mathematics. He was also very agile and gained a blue for gymnastics. In the summer he liked to travel to France and Italy which he did for many years, and in so doing he developed a taste for European literature: Jean Giono and D'Annunzio in particular. He was also very keen on birdwatching. Jarmain graduated in 1933 and a year later he married Eve Houghton whom he had met at Cambridge; she was an art student who had been through the Royal Academy. They moved to Somerset and lived at first in Pilton and then in a small cottage at West Pennard near Glastonbury. They had two children, Mark and Joanna. Jarmain spent most of his time writing novels and poetry and was known locally as something of a recluse. The one novel that eventually saw the light of day, *Priddy Barrows*, was about an eccentric school for boys set on top of Mendip.

Finances were tight and so by 1937 Jarmain had found work as a schoolmaster at Millfield in Street, teaching Mathematics, English Literature and Italian. The now famous *avant-garde* school had been founded only two years previously in 1935 with seven Indian boys, six of whom were princes. 'The Boss' – Jack Meyer – approved of John Jarmain. He was obviously an intelligent communicator who had a particular gift for teaching. John Jarmain enjoyed life to the full and his restless intelligence was always seeking new places and new writers.

But by 1938, things were not going too well at home, his wife Eve was very depressed and John, who had a roving eye, was starting to fix his attention on a younger woman, one Beryl Butler who sometimes stayed up the road in Pilton

edars, which was a small farm owned by her uncle
ʌton who worked for the family firm, United Dairies.

ɛryl Butler, when not in Pilton, lived in Broadstone
neaɪ Poole in Dorset and was very keen on poetry and
literature and had started writing stories. She had heard
about John Jarmain from Reg Lawton's daughter Carol and
cheekily Beryl sent him some stories and poems to look at.
He gave her some good advice and eventually they met in
his small cottage in December 1935 and a rich
correspondence started. Correspondences are very
dangerous things indeed. In 1938 John sought a divorce
from Eve. Then after war was declared in September 1939,
he immediately joined up and eventually, after some hard
training on Salisbury Plain, became a young artillery officer.
He managed to get a week's leave before being posted to
Scotland and married Beryl Butler in Salisbury Registry
Office on 10 May 1940 – the very same day that Hitler
chose to invade France and Belgium. Immaculate timing.

Like many volunteers in the Second World War, John
Jarmain was an unlikely candidate as an army officer. He was
essentially a pacifist like his hero, Jean Giono, who had been
through the horror of the trenches; but Jarmain believed
that this war was necessary. He even had 'atheist' written on
the dog tags which always hung around his neck and said
jokingly, 'I don't suppose God will take a blind bit of notice.'
He served with the famous 51st Highland Division
throughout their campaigns in North Africa and Sicily.

It all came to an end four years later, just before first
light on a June morning in 1944, in a once beautiful
Normandy village surrounded by cider orchards in the

Calvados region just east of Caen, a village that had been severely hammered in the preceding two weeks. A lone jeep drove down the long straight road that dipped into what remained of St Honorine la Chardonnorette (which translates as St Honorine the Goldfinch). Of the seven or eight old farmhouses, hardly a wall was left standing. The whole place had been fought over for two weeks and the air stank of putrefying cattle that had been dead for twelve days and had become obscenely bloated in the summer sun.

John Jarmain was a keen and dedicated battery commander who had come down to see his men before it all 'hotted up'. He thought it was going to get 'sticky' and that there would be a strong counter-attack from the Panzers. He wanted to wish his men good luck before the battle. He would then return to Ranville for a quick breakfast and hand over to his second-in-command, Captain John Kaestlin, who had also been at Cambridge. Some tanks were manoeuvring into position in the half light and making a bit of a racket. There was a traffic jam at the crossroads so Jarmain got out of the jeep and walked forward to reach his men who were dug in behind their anti-tank guns. First light is favourite time to attack.

Then the German mortars started up, the Nebelwerfers or 'Moaning Minnies' as they were called. Jarmain's driver stayed where he was because he was not allowed to leave his vehicle, even under heavy fire. Jarmain, who was by now walking on his own, instinctively made a dash up a slope towards a slit trench; but before he got there, he was hit in the back of the neck by sharp fragments from a mortar bomb.

The officer's personal driver, Lance Bombardier John Lambie, survived the attack. A Glaswegian, John Lambie was also Jarmain's batman and they had been through many scrapes together. Since October 1942 they had been through the battles of El Alamein as well as several other hard-fought skirmishes such as Mersa Brega, Misurata, Leptis Magna, Tripoli, the Mareth Line, Wadi Akrit, Enfidaville; and then had come the invasion of Sicily, Vizzini, Ramacca, Gerbini and the battles in the Sferro Hills. They had driven thousands of miles together in the desert and Lambie's trumpet-playing in the evening, whether it was Tiger Rag or Handel, had kept his officer in the very best of moods. Lambie had even led a dance band in Sicily when they were leaving that colourful island under the shadow of Mount Etna, and the wine had been flowing.

But now it was very different. It was raining and a day or two before, a group of thirty-five Panzer tanks had attacked the village and been beaten off with heavy casualties on both sides. The Panzers were expected to return at any moment and were spotted south west of the village preparing to attack. In amongst them were some heavily armoured and lethal Tiger Tanks.

Ten days earlier Jarmain had helped retrieve three other anti-tank guns from St Honorine which had been abandoned when the infantry had been driven back. The following day, Jarmain and Lambie had both come face-to-face with a Panzer Mark IV; and a jeep is no match for a Panzer. The Panzer fired and luckily the shot missed. The Panzer was hit a few minutes later by one of Jarmain's own anti-tank guns manned by men from Oban and the west coast of Scotland, some no doubt speaking to each other in their native Gaelic. Those new 17-pounder anti-tank guns and 6-pounders were much better than the earlier 2-pounders which were nothing more than pea shooters whose rounds had bounced off the tanks at anything beyond two hundred yards. The 6-pounder was a good gun but still no match for the Tiger Tank which weighed in at 50 tons and had 7 inches of armour plate.

It all came down to ranges and types of shell and depth of enemy armour, although you could always try shooting the tracks off a tank. These heavier guns could penetrate a tank at 800 yards or more. The new 17-pounder guns could really pack a punch and once the tanks were brewed up, the crew had little chance. They were either burnt alive, killed by shrapnel or machine gunned as they emerged from their burning turrets. It was kill or be killed; and the fighting in Normandy in the orchards and hedgerows that summer was very bitter indeed. No quarter was given or taken. Many of these Panzer commanders had trained on the eastern front against the Russians and were very adept at finding and using cover before attacking.

Much of the fighting took place at night. The 61st Anti-Tank Regiment and their guns were often situated right up in the front line alongside the infantry to protect them against tanks. Here at St Honorine, the 5th Cameron Highlanders had paid a very heavy price indeed for capturing the village. In two attacks they had lost half their officers and a quarter of their men, mostly to machine gun fire and mortars. It was like the First World War: a massacre. The village had been finally retaken with a 'silent' attack carried out at three o'clock in the morning helped enormously by the 13th/18th Hussars in their Sherman tanks.

The 51st Highland Division – which had been reformed after the debacle and humiliating surrender at St Valery-en-Caux in 1940 – was made up not just of Cameron Highlanders, but also of Seaforth Highlanders, the Black Watch, the Gordon Highlanders and the Argyll and Sutherland Highlanders, all of whom were recruited from specific parts of the highlands. With their kilts, their skirling pipes and their bayonets glinting in the moonlight, they had in the Western Desert put the fear of God into the German and Italian soldiers. They were known to the Germans as 'The Ladies from Hell.' What the Egyptian and Libyan camels, donkeys, nomadic shepherds and goat boys thought of the pipes and kilts is not known. But the pipes were very effective at keeping the Scottish soldiers' morale up when walking through minefields littered with booby traps and barbed wire, covered with heavy machine gun fire. The regimental pipers took heavy casualties themselves; and several kept playing even after they had been wounded or had had their legs shot off.

In the half light, Lance Bombardier Lambie found Major John Jarmain lying at the side of the road and carried him to the RAP, the Regimental Aid Post, which was dug in close by. Jarmain, the Battery Commander of 193 Battery, was by now unconscious and badly wounded. He was quickly evacuated to the Dressing Station, but he did not survive the journey.

So it was on 26 June 1944 that John Jarmain died, with a piece of mortar shell embedded in the base of his skull.

He had written his last long letter to his wife only a few hours earlier and had stayed up chatting to Captain John Kaestlin about friends at Cambridge and also discussing the battery almost man by man as if handing it over. Maybe, after the narrow squeak with the Panzer, he had had a premonition about his own end. John Jarmain was only thirty three years old.

He left behind a book of poems and the novel *Priddy Barrows* which were both published by Collins to wide acclaim after his death. There was also a clutch of over 150 letters written to his wife Beryl, mostly from the Western Desert, which have only re-surfaced following Beryl's death in a car crash near Swanage in 1990. They were discovered in Jarmain's writing desk by their daughter Janet Susan; and it was ten years until she could bring herself to read them. Janet had been born in August 1942, just before El Alamein. It is these letters, as much as the poems, which are his legacy, for within them he sent back the poems from the front line.

Yet John Jarmain – because of censorship – gives very little away in his letters; and it is often only by reconstructing his army wartime career through the War Diaries of his regiment, and more particularly of the Highland Infantry regiments with whom he served, that a real picture of what he went through begins to emerge. For instance, he often comments on birds that he has seen, but does not mention that a battle is going on at the same time. There were skylarks and the odd ring plover at El Alamein, coursers at Mersa Brega and blue rollers at Enfidaville. He sometimes used birds as clues as to where he might be.

No one knows an officer better than his driver or batman, and to be a hero in their eyes is no easy matter; for living cheek by jowl day after day, they see every imperfection of your soul. Jarmain was in Lambie's eyes 'a very brave man' and in a letter to Jarmain's wife, he wrote, 'One cannot easily forget such a fine man.' Praise indeed. At one point in the desert Jarmain had lent Lambie a copy of *Alice in Wonderland* and eventually after some encouragement Lambie had read it and had been 'converted', though he wasn't sure if he 'should be enjoying a children's book'.

Interestingly, *Alice in Wonderland* was the favourite book of another war poet who had carried it with him through the Western Desert and who was also killed in Normandy by a fragment of mortar bomb – Keith Douglas. They never met or even knew of each other's existence as far as we know, but Keith Douglas was originally commissioned into the 2nd Derbyshire Yeomanry which was allocated to the 51st Highland Division and served with them throughout the various campaigns. For some reason Douglas was transferred in October 1941 to the Sherwood Rangers Yeomanry and served with them in Palestine; otherwise their paths might well have crossed many times.

Military historians estimate that about 70% of casualties in Normandy were from mortar shells: either 81mm or Nebelwerfers, both of which were accurate and effective. In a strange reversal of the Norman invasion, Normandy was taking its toll on the English yet again. Two very fine poets had been silenced within days of each other. Keith Douglas had been killed on tank reconnaissance near

Bayeux on 9 June and is buried in the cemetery at Tilly-sur-Seulles. John Jarmain is buried in the 6th Airborne cemetery at Ranville. Yet both men had been shaped and forged by the desert and their poetry reflects that harshness and isolation into which they retreated when there was a lull in the fighting. They were kindred spirits.

Keith Douglas is now well-known and quite rightly recognised as the best of the Second World War poets. And yet John Jarmain, although not as prolific, is hardly known at all and has yet to be discovered and appreciated by a much wider audience. He was in a sense Douglas's shadow. Douglas was tank; Jarmain was anti-tank. Jarmain was Cambridge; Douglas was Oxford. Jarmain read Mathematics and Douglas read English. Jarmain was married (twice, and had children); Douglas was single. Jarmain wrote a novel; Douglas wrote a war diary. Douglas is well-known – Jarmain hardly known at all.

These two poets have the nature of war well within their grasp. They lived in the front line. They knew what killing meant. They knew what being a soldier meant and the risks that it involved. Their words, their narratives, their poetry, are all we now have to measure them by. And to understand them we have to understand what sort of war it was they were fighting.

John Jarmain wrote about two dozen poems which would count as war poems. One of his first, 'Thinking of War', was written in June 1939 and anticipates his own death even before he had joined up, and a full three months before war had even been declared. Then in Scotland whilst training he describes a man ploughing with horses on the Black Isle. Then there are the war poems which are descriptive but rarely mention the war directly. Some lines jump out at you, such as:

Then in a callow dawn we stood in lines
Like foreigners on bare and unknown quays,
Till someone bravely into the hollow of waiting
Cast a timid wisp of song...

EMBARKATION

Water, which for our thirst is measured out
Each day to every one
From stained and travelled tins with battered edges...

MIRAGE

There are flowers now, they say, at Alamein;
Yes, flowers in the minefields now...

EL ALAMEIN

This is the cool hour I wish to keep,
So I lean toward the moon to write these lines
Before I sleep.

BIVOUAC

Tel-el-Eisa is Jesus' Hill,
Or so they say:

There the bitter guns were never still,
Throwing up yellow plumes of sand by day...

TEL-EL-EISA

We have seen sand frothing like the sea
About our wheels,
Clouds rolling and opaque...

Then with sore lips we cursed the sand,
Cursed this sullen gritty land...

And we have seen wonders, spinning towers of sand...
Lakes where no water was...

Yet sand has been kind for us to lie at ease,
Its soft-dug walls have sheltered and made a shield.

SAND

He's overhead now; keep down...

Listen, he's coming back — I am afraid
I want to live, and now I am afraid.

FEAR

But this burst house with smoking twisted stair,
These scattered limbs in fields of asphodel,
These are an end whose beginning is elsewhere...

BEGINNINGS

Sadly, John Jarmain did not see the end of the war, or even his novel or poems in print. His death must have been very hard indeed for his wife Beryl who was seven months pregnant with twins when he was killed. All that promise felled by a single bit of shrapnel in an attack that never materialised.

Several of Jarmain's poems are in well-known Salamander Oasis anthologies but there is much more to the man than just these few poems. Maybe it is time now to reassess this fine young writer and his unusual contribution to poetry written during the Second World War. A full biography will follow...

JAMES CROWDEN, OCTOBER 2012

QUIET

I will be quiet now, as quiet as prayer.
My heart lays down its songs; all music fails;
For the limits of silence are crossed and in this hour
The simple loveliness alone prevails.
I will be quiet as a worshipper;
For my astonished heart is very still
Before your truth, and all its songs are poor
Since you have led me to your holy hill.

In you my whispered songs have met defeat
And found humility; my hectic vow
Is shamed and empty at so great a thing.
I have no gift to offer at your feet,
O love! — Since all my words are nothing now,
Accept the simple silence that I bring.

.

14-18 MARCH 1938

WAR

Shall we again believe that we fight for right
That peace is sown in the waste red fields of pain?
Shall we keep men's love and truth and honour bright,
And cleanse the world, by murder once again ?

Shall we make war for peace? For life make death,
And for the love of life intently kill? —
By poison gas and the spattered coughing breath
Defend the laws of peace, and man's goodwill?

But we shall have heroes ! — Shoot their lungs away,
Splinter their limbs, with iron burst their eyes.
We shall keep their memory each year. And they,
They will be dead, they will not criticize.

W.P. (WEST PENNARD, 1 APRIL 1936

PLOUGHING ON THE BLACK ISLE

Over the pale field plodding evenly
Two heavy horses draw the simple plough,
Heavy and slow, with the strength of their heavy quarters
Driving against the earth;
The bent ploughman follows, shuffling his steps,
Gruffly muttering to his beasts to keep them moving —
"Come along now, gentlemen," "Come away wi' ye now"
Phrases and words that the wind wraps away.
Slowly, patiently slowly they move up the hillside,
The two slow-moving beasts and the man behind,
The man with his dark hands guiding the plough,
Small and thickset in the wind of the grey day,
Bent-shouldered, wearing an old blue jersey.

They cut the new furrow from the colourless grass,
Cutting along the straight edge they have made,
The edge of the widening bend of brown-turned earth
Where soon the seed will be laid;
Slowly they mount the hillside striped by their ploughing,
Striped new-rich-brown and grey-green in broad bands,
Toward the belt of Scots firs on the ridge
Which hold away the wind from the north.
Behind them is the sad sea, broken by the wind,
Restless, whipped to white wavelets by the wind,
Grey, unhappy, unfruitful.

And the seagulls!
They follow in a circle about the ploughman's head,
Over his hands, around him, after the plough,
Wheeling and calling in circles; hundreds of them,
Dipping and settling in the long straight cut of the furrow,
Rising again, curving and circling and diving.
They are like a white wake of heavy-flying foam,
Heavy-falling foam following the passage of the plough
And lying like a white wake of great white bubbles in a
straight line behind it;
Then rising, screaming, circling after the man again,
Following him like a cloud.
How white, how curving, how restless and vocative they are,
These white circling birds like a cloud from the sea,
Who follow the slow horses and the trudging patient man.

AVOCH, APRIL 1941

THESE POEMS

You who in evenings by the fire
May read these words of mine,
How let you see the desert bare
In the print-smooth line?

Listen! These poems were not made in rooms,
But out in the empty sand,
Where only the homeless Arab roams
In a sterile land;

They were not at tables written
With placid curtains drawn,
But by candelight begotten
Of the dusk and dawn.

They had no peace at their reation,
No twilight hush of wings;
Only the tremble of bombs, the guns' commotion,
And destructive things.

MARETH, TUNISIA, MARCH 1943

EMBARKATION, 1942

In undetected trains we left our land
At evening secretly, from wayside stations.
None knew our place of parting; no pale hand
Waved as we went, not one friend said farewell.
But grouped on weed-grown platforms
Only a few officials holding watches
Noted the stealthy hour of our departing,
And, as we went, turned back to their hotel.

With blinds drawn down we left the things we know,
The simple fields, the homely ricks and yards;
Passed willows greyly bunching to the moon
And English towns. But in our blindfold train
Already those were far and long ago,
Stored quiet pictures which the mind must keep:
We saw them not. Instead we played at cards,
Or strangely dropped asleep.

Then in a callow dawn we stood in lines
Like foreigners on bare and unknown quays,
Till someone bravely into the hollow waiting
Cast a timid wisp of song;
It moved along the lines of patient soldiers
Like a secret passed from mouth to mouth
And slowly gave us ease;

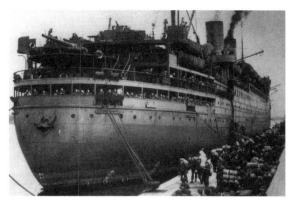

SS *DUCHESS OF RICHMOND*, THE TROOPSHIP
THAT IN 1942 CARRIED JOHN JARMAIN, HIS BATTERY
AND 5,000 TROOPS OF THE HIGHLAND DIVISION
FROM LIVERPOOL VIA CAPETOWN TO PORT TEWFIK
IN EGYPT ©IMPERIAL WAR MUSEUM (NA109)

In our whispered singing courage was set free,
We were banded once more and strong.
So we sang as our ship set sail,
Sang our own songs, and leaning on the rail
Waved to the workmen on the slipping quay
And they again to us for fellowship.

SLEEPING ON DECK

I lie and look at the stars that rock and sway
In a swinging arc beyond the pointer mast
And stiff black spars; I hear from far away
The quiver of the engines' humming song.
And nearer the wave of the white wash hissing past.
Warm as your breath, and fresh, and blowing strong,
The smooth wind fans my eyelids and my hair
And faintly flaps the blankets of my bed.
How still it is! O, my heart has need of you here,
And the hollow of your arm to lay my head.

FLYING FISHES

At first they are like gnats or like a flight of arrows,
Quick and skimming over the water
Brilliantly this way and that way,
Criss-cross like a glimmer of twitched threads.
Then at a moment as they come nearer
I see that they are fishes: or are they birds?
— Bird fishes with fins which are wings,
Dark, pointed, gliding, swallow-like wings
Flashing white on the undersides.
Underwater they have sharp fins striking strongly,
Driving them to speed so that they leave the water flying,
Released like an arrow. Then the fins become wings,
No longer fins but narrow bird-wings in the air,
Then they spread them, dark and pointed and white below,
Spread them and glide, thread the air with them.
(Do they prefer the air, I wonder,
The flicked bright gliding through the air?
Or the flowing half-light of the water,
Swimming with their wings turned fins again
Through the green cave-shadows of the water?)
Look, they are playing these tiny bird-fishes,
Playing all day:
Chasing, skimming, streaming over the water,
They glide, flick the surface, ricochet,

Dart off again and away,
Playing at ducks and drakes;
Finally they fold their wings and fall,
Plop! Clumsily back into the water.
Black and white and glistening
With the pale phospher-sheen on their undersides,
They are like martins flickering over a pool,
Gliding on their narrow wings
Which are black with the white undersides
Like the wings of house-martins at home in England
Like martins over an English pond in June, before rain,
They flicker and skim narrowly over the water,
Low and brilliant over the surface.
But at the pond's edge the martins swoop up again,
Rise and soar into the sun:
These do not soar, they fall back, plop! into the water:
They are only fishes.

IN ALEXANDRIA

A bat slipped past my face
In the street at dusk,
In Alexandria.
It flittered by silently, aimlessly,
Like a flat leaf blown on the wind;
And it had no thickness,
Like a large leaf painted on a teacup.
— Or perhaps it was not a bat:
Perhaps it was the blown residue of a spell,
Made by the old man in a soiled white robe
Who stood muttering on the corner —
I do not know. It did not touch me:
Only the cool wind touched my face.

EL ALAMEIN

There are flowers now, they say, at Alamein;
Yes, flowers in the minefields now.
So those that come to view that vacant scene,
Where death remains and agony has been
Will find the lilies grow —
Flowers, and nothing that we know.

So they rang the bells for us and Alamein,
Bells which we could not hear:
And to those that heard the bells what could it mean,
That name of loss and pride, El Alamein?
— Not the murk and harm of war,
But their hope, their own warm prayer.

It will become a staid historic name,
That crazy sea of sand!
Like Troy or Agincourt its single fame
Will be the garland for our brow, our claim,
On us a fleck of glory to the end:
And there our dead will keep their holy ground.

But this is not the place that we recall,
The crowded desert crossed with foaming tracks,
The one blotched building, lacking half a wall,
The grey-faced men, sand powdered over all;
The tanks, the guns, the trucks,
The black, dark-smoking wrecks.

So be it: none but us has known that land:
El Alamein will still be only ours
And those ten days of chaos in the sand.
Others will come who cannot understand,
Will halt beside the rusty minefield wires
And find there — flowers.

MARETH, TUNISIA, MARCH 1943

from Capt. J. Jarmain. 242/61. A/Tk. Bty. R.A., M.E.F.
No 33   Dec. 8. 1942.

For Alemein

They rang the bells for us, for Alemein:
From church to church across the grassy land
By elm-girt square and tranquil village green
— As there gun answered gun across the sand —
Proudly its grey spires passed the peal
For us, for Alemein. That name will stand,
Long after us maybe, for brave deeds done,
For stubborn glory, and its battle won —
Not for the place we know, its barren shore,
The lonely road amid a   waste of sand
And one sole building   — shed or railway-store —
Whitewashed, and blotted with the crazy scars
Of many bursting shells.

We could not hear the ringing of the bells;
And some, who keep that lonely battle-scene
Will never know they rang. But they alone
In their great quiet possess that land,
And in the silence of the desert sand
What bells are rung for them, for Alemein?

RING PLOVER AT EL ALAMEIN

Nothing grows on the sand-flats
Beside the salt lake at El Alamein;
The water is still and rust-pink
And the flat sand-rim is crusted with salt.
Beyond the white dunes and shallow beach
Is the tideless brilliant sea;
Behind is the desert sand.
Day after day of sand, with not one tree
Yet here at the dead lake's side
Today I saw a solitary ring plover,
Small and plump and coloured
— Black and white and red —
Surprising as a toy of painted wood.
He and I alone were in that flat pale place,
I still and watching him;
Yet he was busy as an absorbed small boy:
He ran importantly, stopped and cocked his head,
Bobbed forward stiffly like a bright mechanical toy,
Small and preoccupied, always hurrying his pace
As if he were always a little behind.

So I have seen him on broad beaches of the North,
Hunting with the dunlin between the fishing-boats
And the nets hung on poles to dry,
Along the shores of the Moray Firth.

But as I watched the quick wings flickered,
Left momentarily a white arc in the air,
And he was over the dunes, out to sea.
I was alone still on the sand-flats
Beside the rust-pink water.

MIRAGE

See how the valley pale with water lies
Silver and shimmering to the early sun
Between the low sand-ridges.
— Water, which for our thirst is measured out
Each day to every one
From stained and travelled tins with battered edges —
But should I walk toward that mocking lake
It would be ever far and ever seen,
Still unattained, still silver-clear and cold,
And I still thirsting — or would part and make
Twin pools, one either side across the sand,
Each still as far. So I should pass between,
Like Moses in the miracle of Old,
Dry, with a magic sea on either hand.

BIVOUAC

In my bivouac at evening lying close
Beneath the tent's low roof,
I steal this moment, quiet on my bed,
To let the dust and wind of day die down
And make still my soul as an evening pool.
Night draws about my head
Her breath of darkness cool,
And at my feet the moon comes palely in:
Like a wan cold field outspread
Is the pale and vacant sand,
Which was so hot and turbid all day long;
And the sky, more mapped with light than any land,
Is filled with all its stars:
The crooked scorpion low across the South
Lies in the tent's small mouth
Like a curled and jewelled snake.
The wind and sand and sounds of day are still,
Now is the desert by the moon washed clean
And pale in beauty shines.
This is the cool hour I wish to keep,
So I lean toward the moon to write these lines
Before I sleep.

SOLDIERS' PRAYER

We do not ask that fate shall mitigate
Whatever hardship we may have to bear.
Nor that we shall not suffer in our share,
Or more, whatever come of wounds and hate:
We do not ask for any recompense
Nor for remembrance in the triumph-day.
Our youth is wasted in its own defence;
Not all your laurels can restore to us
The years that are taken away
With every untouched promise that they bore.
Only we pray that when the guns cease fire
We may return, and not find all things changed.
That then in answer to our heart's desire
We find love waiting, that we feared estranged.

.

SANDBAGS

How does the moon put beauty on the earth,
Exalting things of smallest worth
With her milk-white magic? —
This corner of a sandbag wall,
Stale and untidy in the yellow noon,
Is changed to beauty by the moon,
Made strange and still,
Most smoothly shaped
Like some old tomb white samite draped
With flat black-shadowed folds.

IN A DUG-OUT 'SOMEWHERE IN EGYPT',
1 NOVEMBER 42

TEL-EL-EISA

Tel-el-Eisa is Jesus' hill,
Or so they say:
There the bitter guns were never still,
Throwing up yellow plumes of sand by day
And piercing the night across.
There the desert telephone's long lonely line expires,
Ends with a tangle of looping wires
And one last leaning cross.

EL ALAMEIN, 26 OCTOBER 1942

AT A WAR GRAVE

No grave is rich: the dust that herein lies
Beneath this white cross mixing with the sand
Was vital once, with skill of eye and hand
And speed of brain. These will not re-arise,
These riches, nor will they be replaced;
They are lost and nothing now, and here is left
Only a worthless corpse of sense bereft,
Symbol of death, and sacrifice, and waste.

EL ALAMEIN, 30 OCTOBER 1942

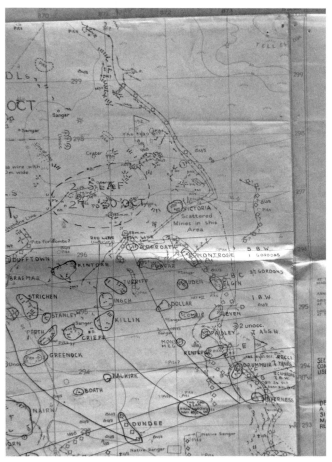

MILITARY MAP OF EL ALAMEIN BATTLEFIELD,
OCTOBER 1942, SHOWING THE START LINE AND
EARLY OBJECTIVES FOR 51ST HIGHLAND DIVISION.
JARMAIN'S BATTERY, 242, WAS ATTACHED TO 152
INFANTRY BRIGADE, WHICH WAS COMPRISED OF
SEAFORTH AND CAMERON HIGHLANDERS..
THE NATIONAL ARCHIVES, REF. WO169/4292

SAND

We have seen sand frothing like the sea
About our wheels, and in our wake
Clouds rolling yellow and opaque,
Thick-smoking from the ground;
Wrapped in the dust from sun and sky
Without a mark to guide them by
Men drove alone unseeing in the cloud,
Peering to find a track, to find a way,
With eyes stung red, clown-faces coated grey.
Then with sore lips we cursed the sand,
Cursed this sullen gritty land
— Cursed and dragged on our blind and clogging way.

We have felt the fevered Khamsin blow
Which whips the desert into sting and spite
Of dry-sand driving rain (the only rain
The parched and dusty sand-lands know,
The hot dry driven sand): the desert floor
Whipped by the wind drives needles in the air
Which pricked our eyelids blind; and in a night,
Sifting the drifted sandhills grain by grain,
Covers our shallow tracks, our laboured road,
Makes false the maps we made with such slow care.

And we have seen wonders, spinning towers of sand
— Moving pillars of cloud by day —
Which passed and twitched our tents away;
Lakes where no water was, and in the sky
Grey shimmering palms. We have learned the sun and stars
And new simplicities, living by our cars
In wastes without one tree or living thing,
Where the flat horizon's level ring
Is equal everywhere without a change.

Yet sand has been kind for us to lie at ease,
Its soft-dug walls have sheltered and made a shield
From fear and danger, and the chilly night.
And as we quit this bare unlovely land,
Strangely again see houses, hills, and trees,
We will remember older things than these,
Indigo skies pricked out with brilliant light,
The smooth unshadowed candour of the sand.

BUERAT-EL-HSUN, JAN. 1943

FEAR

Crouch in the corner of the sandy wall,
Keep below ground;
Wait, and try not to hear.
Forget the evil sound
Drumming in the dark, coming near, coming near.
He's overhead now; keep down.
Passed! — No, he's turning round;
He's coming back over here — This is fear.
Don't keep waiting for it, for the whistling fall,
Then the sick thud. Try not to hear.
In all this sand a man's very small after all.
Think of easy and pleasant things:
No, not of her; not of things too dear —
Think of tomorrow and breakfast and the sun
(A cigarette would show, he's so damned low):
Think of trees, and the brave road curved across the hill
Leading to Tavistock, where lace is made
And speech is soft to hear — That one was near!
The earth is upheaved and trembles down the wall;
Pattering the splinters fall
Listen, he's coming back — I am afraid
I want to live, and now I am afraid.

NOFILIA, EAST OF SIRTE

THE DESERT ARMY

We sailed across the seven seas to fight there
From every continent and each free land;
We brought to dust an empire's boasted might there,
And crossed two thousand miles of desert sand.
Tripoli, Tunis, these our battle honours,
El Alamein, Bir Hacheim and Tobruk;
These are the ribbons that are pinned upon us,
And their names are written in the golden book.

Yet not by the lands we conquered will you know us,
Nor by our battles, though their fame is known;
Not by the powers that came to overthrow us
And failed, and by our strength were overthrown.
For with a greater than armies we contended
— The desert — and that too we overcame:
And the desert will live in us when war is ended;
Though we forget, we shall not be the same.

Though we of the desert army be divided
And find new glory in another land,
Yet,when the sum of battles is decided,
We shall be still the soldiers of the sand.
Then by this you shall know us whereso'er you find us,
In Bombay, Capetown, Auckland or Southend,
That we have a subtle separate pride to bind us,
And each one of us an army for his friend.

We lived outside the world, beyond the borders
Of the lands men use, and there we learned our pride;
With only our battle kit and our marching orders
We learned to make do, and took empires in our stride.
We had for all our company each other
(In the desert let no man dare to stand alone)
Till we were one company, each man a brother:
By this we conquered, by this shall we be known.

MEDENINE, TUNISIA, MARCH 1943

A PIPER OF THE 5TH CAMERONS LEADING HIS
COMRADES ALONG THE ROAD NEAR AGHELIA,
19 DECEMBER 1942
© IMPERIAL WAR MUSEUMS (E 20356)

ORCHIDS

Someone suddenly sang in the darkness
In the empty desert night;
He sang for company as he shovelled the sand,
Digging himself a shelter for the night.
In the bare cold sand and singing of orchids.
And at once in the darkness I saw them,
Orchids,
Green and fungus-yellow and spotted ones,
Fantastically winged and pouting,
Sticky-seeming like shapes of wax
With sprouting pale antennae.

Are these flowers with the sticky waxen petals?
They are not appropriate to fields nor to memory,
But are held between the fingers of fat gentlemen
Or fixed in the hair of slim girls in ballrooms.
Even here in this desert where a flower would be wonder,
Even here I wish for none of them.

But I will remember purple orchids,
Early purples in the fields above Cheddar,
With spotted orchids among them: —
Small pointed trumpets on a tiny stem
(Flowers fading to pink in the sun of Summer),
With the rusty-black spotted green leaves.
These are flowers for a song, grown of the fields,
These I will remember.

9 NOVEMBER 1942

THE BOMBING OF TOBRUK HARBOUR ON
1 SEPTEMBER 1941. THE PORT WAS LITTERED WITH
SUNKEN SHIPS © IMPERIAL WAR MUSEUMS (E 5128)

TOBRUK

Pale as an aquatint, upon the hill
The white town stands beside its deep-blue bay;
Its slender minaret is shimmering still,
And in its gardens, brought from far away
And fostered in the sand with exiles' care,
Are flowers of Italy: magnolias there,
Fuschia and cyclamen and pale-green vines,
Made at the edge of the dry encroaching sand
In this quiet colony a memory,
An image of the green Italian land
Or some steep fishing-port of Sicily.

And now, Tobruk is now a name
And sacked and burned, like Troy.
Its little harbour holds a hundred ships
Which brave with cargoes came,
Whose broken leaning masts like crazy posts
Jut from the tranquil surface of the bay:
Its trim white walls are crumbled, and its flowers
Buried by rubble of bombs; along its streets,
Where fame has strewn this debris and decay
Moves the remembered band of alien ghosts.

MERSA BREGA, LIBYA, 15 DECEMBER 1942

NEW YEAR, 1943

Only the quiet stars and the cold pale sand,
The muffled sound of the sea and no sound else;
Tall and alone and silently I stand,
A man, the shadow in an empty place,
And watch the stars and linger for a sign
At the changing of the years.
A sign? What in the far cold fields of space
Will mark my alternating hopes and fears?
What different hour is this? What is an hour?
(A mark upon the hours, upon the waves,
As if on the sky's arch we had pricked a line
To part the years and mark the changing hour,
And as Orion or the Sisters passed
We made a notch on time: — Here ends the last,
Here shall the new begin.)

Only the many stars, the cold pale sand,
And the changing years; with these silences I stand,
A shape of shadow in an empty place,
And make my lonely sign: —
Not to the year to come, the year that's gone,
Nor to the unimpassioned fields of space,
But for myself, because the tale runs on;
Because in this notch of time on the small round earth,
Quite close across a little friendly sea
One like myself has watched and answers me.

EL AGHEILA, JANUARY 1943

LEPTIS MAGNA

I had my hair cut at Leptis Magna.
(That is the fact, the statement I wish to make.)

Among the white sandhills is a city
Built before Christ was born.
A city standing between the oasis and the sea
And looking northward across the Mediterranean,
Northward toward imperial Rome;
A city of intricately carved tall stone arches
(Work of the Phoenicians these, before men came from Rome),
Of marble columns green-veined and smooth as glass
And floors of tessellated marble from Ferrara,
Fetched in Roman ships, before Christ was born.
The great paving-stones of its streets
Are worn smooth by many feet,
Sandalled feet of nobles, bare feet of slaves;
It had its amphitheatre and theatres,
Its colonnaded market and temples,
Swimming-pools, and a great gymnasium,
All furnished with statues in marble
Of Caesar and the appropriate gods.
And all these great proud buildings,
Planned with magnificence, built to endure,
Were paid for — so the inscriptions insist —
By the moneys of the Lepticans themselves.

TROOPS OF 51ST HIGHLAND DIVISION VIEWING THE
RUINS AT LEPTIS MAGNA
© IMPERIAL WAR MUSEUMS (E21834)

How greatly they planned, how lavishly,
How well they built their city, these Lepticans,
Taking for model the mother of cities,
Fetching their marble from Ferrara, across the sea;
They must have been proud in their city, and justly.
But they fell into the oblivion of time, the Lepticans,
And their city was buried beneath the sand.

Only now have men come again from Rome to Leptis,
Lovingly have removed the sand of fourteen centuries,
Uncovered the pavements and the Phoenician arches,
The great green-veined marble columns
(Still standing, enduring, still smooth as glass),
And all the beauty purchased by the Lepticans.
I sat on a German petrol-tin among the sandhills
While a small fat Jew cut my hair.
As the snippets fell and strayed on the white sand
I saw the ants come out, big with black dumb-bell bodies,
Carrying them off for their own purposes,
Burrowing in the white African sand.

The ants, the shreds of my hair, the buried city
(Passed and a fable now, the glory of the Lepticans),
They are all disconnected, irrelevant one to another,
Incongruous. So I found them; so I have set them down.

PRISONERS OF WAR

Like shabby ghosts down dried-up river beds
The tired procession slowly leaves the field;
Dazed and abandoned, just a count of heads,
They file away, these who have done their last,
To that great safety where the days are sealed,

Where no word enters, and the urgent past
Is relieved day by day against the clock
Whose hours are meaningless, whose measured rate
Brings nearer nothing, only serves to mock.

It is ended now. There's no more need to choose,
To fend and think and act: no need to hate.
Now all their will is worthless, none will lose
And none will suffer though their courage fail.
The tension in the brain is loosened now,
Its taut decisions slack: no more alone
— How I and each of us has been alone
Like lone trees which the lightnings all assail —
They are herded now and have no more to give.

Even fear is past. And death, so long so near,
Has suddenly receded to its station
In the misty end of life. For these will live,
They are quit of killing and sudden mutilation;
They no longer cower at the sound of a shell in the air,
They are safe. And in the glimmer at time's end
They will return — old, worn maybe, but sure —
And gather their bits of broken lives to mend.

SICILY, AUGUST – OCTOBER, 1943

A GROUP OF 258 GERMAN PRISONERS TAKEN BY THE
BLACK WATCH AT EL ALAMEIN, NOVEMBER 1942.
THIS PHOTOGRAPH WAS FOUND IN JOHN JARMAIN'S
OWN PHOTOGRAPH ALBUM AND MAY WELL HAVE
INSPIRED HIS POEM 'PRISONERS OF WAR'
© IMPERIAL WAR MUSEUM (E18691)

MAJOR JARMAIN R.A., 1944

FAILURE

It is not death nor destiny nor age
Nor any such superb antagonist
That works the soul's defeat, and scrawls the page
With projects turned aside, high aims dismissed,
And blurred and fingered hope. By fate opposed
Men prove their purpose, in the dangerous hour
Their brief excelling brilliance is disclosed:
When threatened most the soul puts forth its flower.

O send me great opponents! Day by day
The precious hours like vacant windows passed,
The petty vision and the soft delay,
These bring defeat and rust the sword we bear,
Diminish each bright purpose; till at last
All's wasted, and the heart's too dull to care.

FEBRUARY 1944

THE INNOCENT SHALL SUFFER

Returning from their traverse of the sky
In the unkind mist of the hour before the dawn,
The young men speak of mortal battles won,
Of cloud-paths and the aiming steady eye,
In clipped and careless phrases. Until one,
Moved by the wonder, told how through the night
Like a gold rose the beaten cities burn;
How in the far perspective of his height
He saw the white heat at the flower's heart glow,
And feathery rings of flaking petals spread
Profuse from each bright centre, till, he said,
No rose in all the earth was blossomed so.

These that go out and sow this burning rose,
Steering their furtive vigil star by star
To send down death, are men of common care;
Each loves and seeks in some girl heart's repose,
Peace on her lips, the respite of her hair.
Yet if, to share his heart, he should confide
This beauty of the cities sown with fire,
Would she not chill and stiffen at his side,
Feeling as woman women there below?
Though boyish still and smilingly he lies
Will she not scan his face with different eyes,
Seeing so clear what he must surely know?

For she that gives him love on his return
Is she that with her lover at her side
Is in her sleep impersonally destroyed,
Whose room has walls of flame. She sees them burn,
The houses which man's hope has slowly made;
She sees them die, the children by the wall,
Old men in pipe-smoke at the chimney-side,
Women who wait alone — these innocent all.
Then in her fear she clasps him to her breast,
Her rich precarious love,
Les death dividing strike them from above
And she not watchful to protect his rest.

Spare then these innocent: loose from the sky
War's total fury on the battlefield,
That poor scarred earth, and leave us undespoiled
The cities of our peace. Let these men die
Who carry arms to be their country's shield,
To serve some abstract, or because they must;
And to their hell that kill or else are killed,
Hiding like outcasts in the threatened dust,
Add this last curse. O earth what deed is this!
What is their guilt who either die or kill
— His life or mine — compelled by equal will
For peace and home and some girl's waiting kiss?
Bare duty speeds their shells, no thought of hate,
And coldly as a man that rules a line

The aimer looses his huge malison
On sleep, whose end he dare not contemplate:
He dare not see, for he must go again,
Again destroy. What man can stop his eyes
And shut his mind to cities red with pain,
— His work — but in his heart compassion dies
And leaves an empty place? What deep-scarred harm
Is cut into the hearts of these who kill,
Whose killing is their work, their only skill,
Whose last pride is a cold and jesting calm
Guilty and innocent both is every one:
Innocent in his own stark suffering,
Guilty in every other suffered wrong.
There is none blameless for the evil done;
For he that scatters death is he that loves,
Is he that loses love and he that grieves
And he that with love's body joined as one
Is by the death cut down: on each that lives
Falls the great guilt of every one that dies.
— Enduring every torment man conceives
How brave is man, who neither fails nor cries!
Knowing the evil, master of the cause,
Yet thrusting the blood-red picture out of mind,
How coward weak and guilty is mankind
Which has not dared forbid what it abhors.

DULLINGHAM, APRIL — MAY 1944

BEGINNINGS

In their beginning, how muddled, loose and crude
Are all great things men make upon the earth;
The painting in a few smudged charcoal lines,
The tall-arched church in awkward stones, not trued,
And heaps of lime and sand and paper plans.
The woman's cries, the pain and blood of birth
For a man first made; the uncouth attitude
And shamefaced lovely lust of his conceiving.

But this burst house with smoking twisted stair,
These scattered limbs in fields of asphodel,
These are an end whose beginning is elsewhere —
In the smooth bright shapely shell
And the great gun lifted gleaming in the air,
Perfect with all the skill of men's contriving.

SILENCES

How good it is to love you! All day long
I have been happy, while the equal hours
Like old slow ships in splendour moved along:
I have been full of quiet as summer flowers.
As quiet as bees: and then you turned your head
And suddenly laughed, like falling golden showers
Of dusky petals, breaking with quick alarm
The stillness we had made. I saw again
That curve your body has of breast and arm,
And all your stirring beauty: bright as pain
Was my desire. This hot astonishment
With flush of flame burns up our quietness —
Then, in a moment freed and crowned and spent,
Draws close the curtains of the silences.

JUNE 1938 – JULY 1939

BARN OWL

Great soft wings, pale and creamy-yellow,
Downy-soft and silent, with long sleepy beat
Slow and lazy-moving in the haze of summer evenings
When silence like a curtain ends the day's long heat;

Fat fluffed-up body with the tiny bones inside it.
Skeleton no bigger than a child's small hand;
Tiny body hidden in the fluffed downy feathers
Slowly sailing, skimming the dusk still land;

Hedge-high he sails with flapping noiseless wing-beats,
Hunts the lines of stubble ready for the plough;
Slowly turns and slowly rises, as if he were too heavy,
Upward planes, and settles on a low elm bough.

In the same silent evenings years ahead in other summers,
When our eyes have drunk the quietness that time passed yields,
Still the owl will fly there, the same one or another,
Big and softly sailing in these or other fields;

Will float hedge-high, hunt the lines of stubble,
With slow flapping flight along the warm dusk air;
And you and I will stand there together in the doorway,
Saying to each other, "Look, the old owl's there.".

AUGUST 1939

A FEW HISTORICAL COMMENTS ON THE POEMS...

by James Crowden

Jarmain is a man of silence and solitude and the war is at first almost a backdrop. Even in his war poems there is scant mention of death and killing; the anti-tank guns are hardly mentioned at all; and of the German tanks, the Panzers, his targets, there is hardly a word, except 'The black, dark smouldering wrecks', as if to mention them would be to tempt fate. Sand of course features quite a bit, as does being dive-bombed by Stukas, which is not a pleasant experience at all. Fear creeps into his poems just like the sand and the asphodels. But Jarmain, one feels, is always observing the war from a slight angle, at one remove, like an ornithologist; and in a sense the war takes second place to his sheer joy at birdwatching, even in the midst of a battle. Just like C.P. Cavafy who lived in Alexandria just 60 miles down the road, he is always thinking of life at a slight tangent. For instance, in early 1943 he is looking back at El Alamein almost nostalgically, even though he is still in North Africa. He is anticipating spring there and the flowers and future visitors who will never comprehend what it is they all actually went through – 'ten days of chaos in the sand'. The 'one blotched building, lacking half a wall' is the obscure railway station that gave the battlefield its name. With 'Orchids' he is looking back to happier times in Somerset on top of the Mendip Hills near Cheddar, and this was written on the eve of the great battle, not knowing whether he would survive or not. In a sense, the orchids and asphodels take the place of First War poppies in his poetry; but the real heroes in his poems and letters are the birds, the skylarks that keep singing even during the intense artillery barrages.

Even in 'Soldiers' Prayer' he is anticipating going home and a soldier's hope that loved ones have not been changed by the war, are not 'estranged'. All the time he is seeking both the company of birds and the desert silence. His liking for solitude is answered here and there; and in 'Bivouac' he is very content leaning towards the moon whilst writing his lines of poetry and finishing off letters that will go back down the line in the morning with the return of the ration truck. The war for Jarmain is in effect a mirage. It is the landscape that he is entranced by, and the fleeting glimpses of birds, whether they be coursers, blue rollers, skylarks or ring plovers. He even finds beauty in the corner of a sandbag in the moonlight.

In 'The Desert Army' his most memorable line is perhaps 'And the desert will live within us when war is ended', which recognises the power of the place, the indescribable solemnity of silence and the vast spaces interspersed with the odd inconvenient battle. He is very much part of the 8th Army: 'Soldiers of sand... We lived outside the world, beyond the borders of lands men use'.

And it is the desert which is the key to his poems; and in a sense you have to have been alone in the desert to understand their understated meaning. A very telling comment about the nature of this particular war comes from a captured German officer who, in conversation with Captain Hamish Henderson, said that 'Africa changes everything. In reality we are allies, and the desert is our common enemy.'

Captain Henderson was the intelligence officer for the 51st Highland Division and would have been known to John Jarmain as he would have attended Henderson's various lectures and briefings on enemy dispositions, strengths, locations and so on. After the war, Henderson's own acclaimed collection of desert poetry was published in a slim volume called *Elegies for the Dead in Cyrenaica*.

John Jarmain manages somehow to keep writing poems and letters even when in the middle of a battle, or rather in any short lull that presents itself. He has his hair cut in 'Leptis Magna', and appreciates the antiquity of the place. He sees lines of prisoners of war being shepherded back behind the front line, 'Like shabby ghosts down dried up river beds/ The tired procession slowly leaves the field'. One poem that escaped the original war poetry section is 'Beginnings'; and it in some ways echoes T.S. Eliot's 'East Coker' which was first published in 1940 and would have been well known to Jarmain. 'In my end is my beginning': this in a sense could apply to Jarmain himself. For in the poem there are echoes of his own creation and destruction: 'the smooth bright shapely shell / And the great gun lifted gleaming in the air, / Perfect with all the skill of men's contriving.' Except in his case, it was a mortar shell that had his name written on it.

Yet even this poem has echoes of Alamein or Mersa Brega where many soldiers were needlessly killed and maimed in minefields: 'These scattered limbs in fields of asphodel'. And also a scene most likely from Sicily after a bombardment: 'This burst house with smoking twisted stair'.

This collection ends with 'Silences' about his wife, and 'Barn Owl' – the rural idyll he never managed to return to, though in the poem he imagines himself there with Beryl in old age. Perhaps he is still out there birdwatching on the Somerset Levels, or roaming in the Western Desert, which to the ancient Egyptians was the land of the hereafter. After death, as spirits, they all 'went west.'

COMMENTS ON INDIVIDUAL POEMS

'THINKING OF WAR'

This is an extraordinary poem because of when it was written. It echoes Rupert Brooke of course, but the date is significant. It is June 1939 and it is three months before war is declared. Jarmain has not yet joined up and yet he is already thinking of his own death and the effect it will have on Beryl Butler. It releases her in advance of his own death and leaves her free to take another. She later married him on 10 May 1940, the day Hitler's armies invaded France.

'QUIET'

This obviously refers to the consummation of his affair with Beryl Butler, possibly within sight of Glastonbury Tor... She would have been 23 and he 27. Maybe they eloped for a short while. In fact they had many illicit liaisons in London where she was working for the well known florist Constance Spry.

'WAR'

This poem, although somewhat simplistic, ponders the morals of war, and was written in West Pennard, Somerset on 1 April 1936. Interestingly the controversial war in Ethiopia, where mustard gas was used indiscriminately against civilians, was coming to an end. The war had been followed very closely in the west and one of the young journalists out there was Evelyn Waugh.

On 31 March 1936 the last big battle was fought between the Ethiopian Army under Haile Selasse and the much better equipped Italian army at Maychew in Tigre province. The Ethiopians attacked first and were gaining ground and about to take the initiative when they were bombed from the air. By the end of the day the Ethiopians had lost nearly 11,000 men. Little did John Jarmain know that within six years he too would be fighting the same Italian forces in the desert. It was Fascism in action on a grand scale and the Italian tactics alarmed many.

1 April 1936 also saw two other important events. The first was that Austria re-introduced military conscription in defiance of the Treaty of St Germain. And to counter this, on the very same day, the British government sent "letters of reassurance" to the Belgian and French governments, assuring them of British support in the event of a future war with Germany. So the die was cast and in a sense so John Jarmain's fate was also sealed. 1 April 1936 was an important day.

The Spanish Civil War was also brewing up quietly behind the scenes and eventually in July 1936 the Spanish Foreign Legion blew a gasket in Morocco and warfare spilled over onto the mainland. John Jarmain was well aware of the dangers that lurked abroad. His best friend at Cambridge and brother-in-law, Michael Barkway, was working at the BBC and edited the World Service and Empire News. So he would have had an inside track on what was really going on in Europe and beyond.

Michael Barkway later worked for 'PsyOps' and PWE, the Political Warfare Executive, on Eisenhower's staff 1944-1945. John Jarmain was therefore very well informed but deep down I suspect he preferred birdwatching and solitude to warfare and politics. Poetry was his outlet.

'PLOUGHING ON THE BLACK ISLE'

This is almost Edward Thomas or Thomas Hardy – not a mention of war, yet they had been training hard in Scotland for nearly a year. The sight of a man and ploughing team with seagulls in pursuit must have reassured Jarmain that all was well with the world. This is a scene that could easily have come from one of Jean Giono's books. In fact to fully understand John Jarmain's view of the world, one has to read the works of Jean Giono. As John Kaestlin remarks about John Jarmain, 'His was a conscious and calculated awareness, the satisfying awareness of Bobi in *Que Ma Joie Remeure*, a book in which he found reflected so much of himself.'

When not training with his guns, Jarmain was living with Beryl in a small cottage at Avoch on the Black Isle. They were frequent guests at the rambling run-down Rosehaugh House, a granite mansion that looked more like a fairytale castle. The drive was full of weeds. It was pulled down in 1959.

'THESE POEMS'

This is a polite warning to the reader, like the warning on a cigarette packet 'Smoking can seriously damage your health.' It tells the reader that these poems were created 'not at tables' but by 'candlelight begotten'; there is 'No twilight hush of wings' as the barn owl glides. Their creation was accompanied only by 'the tremble of bombs, the guns' commotion'. Beware their simplicity. Learn to read between the lines. This poem was written in March 1943 in front of the Mareth Line, a vast concrete fortification armed to the teeth, a bit like the Maginot line but in French Tunisia.

'EMBARKATION'

They left Aldershot by train at night and arrived in Liverpool Docks on 20 June 1942 when they boarded the requisitioned liner *SS Duchess of Richmond* – one of the 'drunken duchesses' that rolled heavily in bad weather. There were about 5,000 troops on board so it was a tight squeeze below decks. This poem captures magnificently the poignancy of troops leaving their homeland shores. Many would never return. John Jarmain shared a cabin with his Battery Commander, Major Harry Dunn. They were in 242 Anti-Tank Battery which was part of 61st Anti-Tank Regiment. Most of the men came from Oban on the west coast of Scotland. The convoy was designated WS20 and was a 'Winston Special'. They sailed north of the Clyde, rendezvoused with other ships off Oransay, sailed south to Freetown and then stopped off in Capetown before sailing up the East Coast of Africa to Aden, the Red Sea and Port Tewfik.

'FLYING FISHES'

This is a finely observed piece on the nature of how flying fishes actually get airborne. As an ornithologist Jarmain must have been fascinated by this. It was written somewhere off the West Coast of Africa and the poem sent from Cape Town.

'SLEEPING ON DECK'

The voyage was largely uneventful and 15,000 miles of steaming took 59 days at an average speed of 14.2 knots with very little smoke. One or two soldiers fell overboard. One died when a submachine gun went off during training and another died of malaria. They also did PT, played bridge, took up boxing and sunned themselves.

'IN ALEXANDRIA'

Having arrived at Port Tewfik in August 1942, the same day Monty took over from Claude Auchinleck, the 51st Highland Division had to start acclimatising to the heat, dust and flies. They spent two months or so in transit camps such as Tahag and Qassasin which were 'hell holes', and then began to exercise in the desert. They even went into the front line on patrol in No Man's Land with Australian troops. It was here that they picked up the slang word *doover* for dugout, and learnt many of the desert ways, not least navigation.

John Jarmain had to attend a court martial in Alexandria. This poem is a minimalist view of the dusk. The German army was only sixty miles up the line. Back in July 1942 during the first battle of El Alamein, the Intelligence departments and diplomatic clerks in Cairo had panicked and burnt all their Top Secret files as they thought Rommel would be amongst the pyramids in a day or two. The sky turned dark as plumes of smoke rose up and bits of charred paper floated down to earth. In Cairo the first of July 1942 was always known as Ash Wednesday.

'EL ALAMEIN'

This is perhaps Jarmain's defining poem which, like 'Embarkation', was published in *The Daily Telegraph*. It was written in front of the Mareth Line in Tunisia and sent back on 16 March 1943, which means that he must have been mulling it over in his mind for a month or two. John Jarmain had a notebook and all his ideas were jotted down in it, usually in pencil, and then worked on when he had time. The battle of Medenine which had occurred on 6 March 1943 was a defensive line opposite the Mareth line; and this was Rommel's last main armoured attack which failed, otherwise known as Operation Capri. The hidden anti-tank guns and artillery held their fire till the very last moment; then all hell let loose, as it had done in Alamein back in October 1942. The Germans lost 52 tanks, a severe blow to their dwindling stocks. John Jarmain wrote the poem 'El Alamein' and sent it back ten days later. Fighting began again on 19 March and continued for nine days. So this poem was written within a very short window. Jarmain was always conscious that he had to get poems off in letters before the next push. In fact two days earlier, one of his good friends, Major Rex Smith, had been reported missing on a recce behind enemy lines. He was killed. Another old friend, Major Donald MacArthur, was wounded in the face. Jarmain was by then in temporary command of 241 Battery.

So these 'rest' periods between battles were anything but rests. All the troops were constantly probing the enemy defences and seeking weak spots, and marking out minefields and gun emplacements.

Here in 'El Alamein', John Jarmain combines the smouldering battlefield scenes with talk about flowers: 'There are flowers now, they say, at Alamein; / Yes, flowers in the minefields now.'

The emphasis is on the words 'now' and 'flowers', both of which are repeated. Interestingly the asphodel lilies, to which he is referring, have a direct connection with Greek mythology, where the 'asphodel meadows' are where the souls of people who lived lives of near equal good and evil rested, a neutral plateau. Obviously a few notches down

FOUR MEN OF THE 51ST (HIGHLAND) DIVISION DUG
IN NEAR EL ALAMEIN, 27 OCTOBER 1942
© IMPERIAL WAR MUSEUMS (E 18625)

from the Elysium Fields. These asphodel flowers were the
favourite food of the Greek dead. It is described as a ghostly
place. Homer describes the plant as being deeply
connected with the underworld. It is often planted on
graves and its link with death is due no doubt to the greyish
colour of its leaves and its yellowish flowers, which suggest
not only the gloom of the underworld but the pallor of
death itself. Persephone, the goddess of vegetation, often
appears with a garland of asphodels. So it is fitting that the
battlefield of El Alamein which saw so much death should
be thus adorned.

CHURCHILL MK III TANKS OF 'KING FORCE' MOVING
FORWARD TOWARDS THE BATTLE AREA DURING THE
SECOND BATTLE OF EL ALAMEIN, 5 NOVEMBER 1942
© IMPERIAL WAR MUSEUMS (E 18989)

In many ways El Alamein was an important victory which was won at very great cost, particularly in the 51st Highland Division where some of the battalion's casualties were as high as fifty percent. Douglas Wimberley, the much admired and celebrated commander of the 51st, said afterwards behind the scenes, 'Never again.' The cost was very high in human life but honour had been restored. Rommel was now in retreat and on the back foot.

Churchill made sure that El Alamein was celebrated in true style and so he gave permission for all the church bells to be rung up and down the country on 15 November 1942, the first time that church bells had been rung since the beginning of the war. But the poem is also about nostalgia and reality. 'The crowded desert crossed with foaming tracks,/ The one blotched building, lacking half a wall,/ The grey-faced men, sand powdered over all;/ The tanks, the guns, the trucks,/ The black, dark-smoking wrecks.'/ ... 'And those ten days of chaos in the sand.'

'RING PLOVER AT EL ALAMEIN'

This was actually written in a letter sent on 13 November, ten days after the battle of El Alamein, but may well refer to an event before that in early October when they were in the front line with Australian troops. El Alamein is close to the sea and there are obviously stretches of salt marsh, beloved of ring plovers, and Jarmain is reminded of ring plovers on the Moray Firth back in Scotland where he trained.

Interestingly, in a letter dated 28 September 1942 he is expressing severe doubts about the nature of war. 'I still believe that the whole process, in which I am participating, is completely useless and valueless, and productive only of suffering and a vast incalculable waste.' Within a week, his battery suffer their first casualties with a tank 'shoot-out'.

The plover signifies bird migration and is a link back to Scotland and home, and the reverse migration of the soldiers who are by now in flocks upon the shores. John Jarmain is trying to keep a grip of his reality by identifying the behaviour of the plover on the shore. 'He and I alone were in that flat pale place,/ I still and watching him;/ Yet he was busy as an absorbed small boy'. This is reminiscent of Norman MacCaig's 'Dipper' but predates it by at least forty years. Norman MacCaig was born in 1910, one year before Jarmain, but did not join up. He was a conscientious objector. If he had served he would almost certainly have been drafted into the 51st Highland Division and been at El Alamein. Another famous Scottish poet from the West Coast who was wounded at El Alamein was Sorley MacLean. He trod on an 'S' mine on 2 November towards the end of the battle and was badly wounded in both feet. He served as a signaller with the Royal Horse Artillery. He wrote in Gaelic.

'MIRAGE'

In a sense, for Jarmain the war was a shimmering mirage. Water was the key to survival and to see it however fleetingly in the desert air must have been tantalising. The reality, however, was 'Water, which for our thirst is measured out/ Each day to every one/ From stained and travelled tins with battered edges…'

'BIVOUAC'

This is a glimpse of John Jarmain's private life within his *doover* or dugout, a small hole in the ground covered with a tent or some such device for keeping the sand and sun out. This is his private intimate world where he writes in the moonlight. 'I steal this moment, quiet on my bed / To let the dust and wind of day die down / And make still my soul as an evening pool.' And there he watches as 'at my feet the moon comes palely in: / Like a wan cold field outspread.' Outside he sees the stars, 'The crooked scorpion low across the South / Lies in the tent's small mouth / Like a curled and jewelled snake.' He is keen to record this scene as if it is a nightly meditation, a solitude

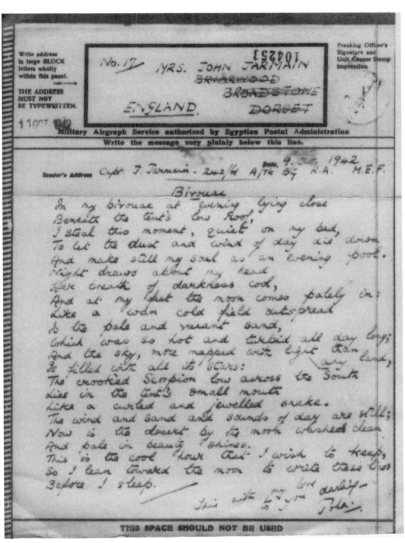

ORIGINAL AEROGRAM OF 'BIVOUAC', 9 OCTOBER 1942

and silence drawn directly from the desert, a deep well from which his writing at last emerges, cautiously and deliberately. 'This is the cool hour I wish to keep,/ So I lean toward the moon to write these lines/ Before I sleep.'

'SOLDIERS' PRAYER'

Here John Jarmain is trying to see things from the soldier's perspective. It is simple, plain and touching, and very relevant to Jarmain's own situation in that the soldier does not want to skip his duty whatever it might be but only asks that his family, his love, his wife, his girlfriend be not estranged because of events which he has gone through or which his loved ones have gone through. It is a grim reality that separation for so long had a disastrous effect on family life. Hence the importance of the mail and letters.

When Monty got to Tripoli he apparently said to Churchill, 'Here's Tripoli for you... now I want something in return...'; and that was a direct air mail letter service back to the UK so that letters to and from his soldiers took only five days. And that boosted morale as much as the Highland pipe bands that marched through the date palms.

'SANDBAGS'

To create a poem about sandbags is something of an achievement. 'This corner of a sandbag wall,/ Stale and untidy in the yellow noon,/ Is changed to beauty by the moon'. Sandbags: the obvious defence for any gun emplacement, just needing the gunny bags and a shovel to fill them. No shortage of sand in the desert. This poem was written whilst the battle of Alamein was still going on and in its stickiest phase right at the very end before the break-out, when every ditch and knoll and fold and slight ridge in the land was challenged by tanks and anti-tank fire, bayonets and snipers. This poem, like many of John Jarmain's, is very much an understatement, and minimalist. What is important is what is happening on the other side of the sandbag during both day and night. Much of the fighting was at night on moonlit nights.

'TEL-EL-EISA'

Tel-el-Eisa is the next station up the line from El Alamein. It is also a small hill to the north west of the station, a feature called Kidney Ridge, which was in fact a depression. Here there was particularly bitter fighting. The battle started on the night of 23 October 1942. They held on desperately to ground they had gained and were hammered during the day and could barely move. The 51st attacked again on the night of 25 October and there were very heavy casualties. By 26 October – the day the poem was actually written – the 51st had advanced six miles and had lost over 2,000 men. The sense of Calvary is all too apparent. 'Tel-el-Eisa is Jesus' Hill,/ Or so they say:/ There the bitter guns were never still,/ Throwing up yellow plumes of sand by day/...one last leaning cross.' The tangled wires symbolise communication at a standstill. Jarmain was also an atheist, so for him this is an interesting poem. Crucifixion, guns and a broken telephone line. A snapshot of war.

'AT A WAR GRAVE'

This was written four days later when the battle was still far from settled. The fighting had reached a stalemate and the impetus of the main attack had stalled. Preparations were underway for a final push; so there was time to bury the dead – the ones that could be found and brought in.

This might be a friend of his, a soldier he knew. Small white wooden crosses appeared everywhere; and with the minefields still active, retrieving bodies was a dangerous job. Later on the bodies were often boobytrapped, so it was a risky business. The sense of sacrifice and waste is all too apparent to Jarmain, though in the end necessary to turn the tide back.

INFANTRYMEN MOPPING UP THE TRENCHES OF THE
MARETH LINE, MARCH 1943
©IMPERIAL WAR MUSEUM (NA1336)

'SAND'

The desert is sand, sand, rocks and dunes. Unremitting heat and at times very cold at night. If conditions are right, then travel can be easy; if the sand is too soft, travel is very slow indeed. One deception that was used was to let maps fall into enemy hands that had 'safe' tracks marked on them that were anything but safe. This was a tactic used at Alam el Halfa in the first week of September 1942 which drew Rommel's tanks into a neatly planned trap. Half the battle was knowing the desert and how to navigate where there were no real landmarks. Many army officers had a copy of Ralph Bagnold's excellent book *Libyan Sands* tucked into their back pockets, as well as one of his sun compasses on the bonnet of their jeep or truck. Ralph Bagnold is credited with founding the LRDG, the Long Range Desert Group, a forerunner of the SAS; and they were a very wild bunch who patrolled behind enemy lines with machine guns mounted on jeeps, gathering intelligence, finding new routes and shooting up supply columns and airfields.

Travelling in the desert was the key. John Jarmain captures it very well indeed. 'We have seen sand frothing like the sea / About our wheels, and in our wake / Clouds rolling yellow and opaque/... Then with sore lips we cursed the sand, / Cursed this sullen gritty land...' But at the same time he was filled with awe at its natural beauty and power: 'And we have seen wonders, spinning towers of sand... / Lakes where no water was...'

And he also credited sand with giving them protection when they needed it: it was a form of protection particularly if you were being dive-bombed by Stukas or suffering from counter-battery fire. 'Yet sand has been kind for us to lie at ease, / Its soft-dug walls have sheltered and made a shield'. Slit trenches and *doovers* were a case in point.

But there was always an air of uncertainty about the desert which Ralph Bagnold touches on in *Libyan Sands*: 'We were a little afraid of the western desert, not so much because it was waterless and entirely uninhabited but because it was different from all experience... The western desert has also always been a land of mystery... There are deserts and deserts...'

'FEAR'

Here John Jarmain is ruthlessly honest about his first experience of an air raid, more than likely a dive-bombing by a Stuka, a Ju 87 which dived at an angle of 60-90 degrees, and reached a speed of about 350 mph with its wailing siren going. They would carry one 250kg bomb under the fuselage and four 50kg bombs, two under each wing so that they could come round a second time; which is exactly what happens in this poem. Once a Stuka picks its target and starts its dive it is very difficult to shoot it down. The main German Stuka airfield was at Sidi Haneish which is about 20 miles from Mersa Matruh. They were often stationed at makeshift airfields very close to the front line and could fly ten sorties a day. The siren was a pair of 'Jericho trumpets' mounted on each wing; and as the plane dived, the rush of air activated the siren which on the ground changed pitch through what is known as the Doppler Effect.

Jarmain sent the poem back in a letter on 11 January 1943 and says this about it:

'This verse that follows almost needs musical directions for reading it (*lento, prestissimo, rallentando* etc.),

A GERMAN JUNKERS JU 87 STUKA DIVE BOMBER
ATTACKING A BRITISH SUPPLY DEPOT NEAR TOBRUK,
LIBYA, OCTOBER 1941

and should only be read aloud; very slowly for the most part, with occasional quicker bits.

'This poem has been in my mind since Alamein. It does refer to a night there; I wrote to you during that night – I wonder whether you can pick the letter? But like all poems the statement has grown in my mind to some extent while waiting to be set on paper.'

'Forget the evil sound / Drumming in the dark, coming near, coming near. / He's overhead now; keep down. / Passed! – No, he's turning round; / He's coming back over here – This is fear… / I want to live, and now I am afraid.' Being dive-bombed was no joke, and the wailing siren didn't help.

What is interesting is that his thoughts about fear and death are – for a moment at least – replaced with thoughts about home; not about his wife, but about certain views they enjoyed on their honeymoon: 'the brave road curved across the hill/ Leading to Tavistock, where lace is made'. The hill is the fine western edge of Dartmoor, and the road is just as striking today as it was then. Honiton was the pre-eminent Devon lace town, but lace still turns up in Tavistock today. It was written at Nofilia which is east of Sirte.

'THE DESERT ARMY'

This was John Jarmain's attempt at a Kiplingesque view of the Desert Army. He sent it on 26 March 1943 from Medenine as the battle was still going on. His view of the 8th Army was characteristically bullish. He obviously enjoyed being a soldier in the desert and admired the desert army for its eccentric and unconventional ways.

As he says in a letter, 'This desert army is unique, it has a character all its own. My division has a sufficiently pronounced character, you would think, but this desert army has a character more definite even than that, and deeper-rooted because it is based on something bigger and more enduring than itself – on the desert.' Views and sentiments which overspill into the poem: 'And the desert will live in us when war is ended;/ Though we forget, we shall not be the same./...We lived outside the world, beyond the borders/ Of the lands men use...'

'ORCHIDS'

This poem also comes from El Alamein and was sent back in a letter dated 9 November 1942, the first letter he wrote after the battle of El Alamein. Here they had been drawn out of the front line briefly to recover from the 'ten days of chaos in the sand.' Jarmain is clearly very shaken by the experience of such a large and bitter battle. He says, 'I am not truly in the mood for letters tonight... but while the battle was in its later stages, moving rapidly, I had no opportunity for writing, and I cannot be sure when I shall have it again. Everything is still so confused in my mind after all the new things, new impressions, and rapid movement, that I cannot sort myself out at all yet.'

The poem was probably written before the battle, possibly on the very eve of battle, shoved into his notebook and left there till they came to rest.

It is of a soldier singing a song about orchids as he digs a slit trench for himself. How poignant those songs must have been, just as poignant as they were when leaving Liverpool on the troopship *SS Duchess of Richmond* back in June. But Jarmain has no time for tropical and exotic orchids; his mind is back in Somerset, with the early purple orchids above Cheddar Gorge. This may well be where he did some of his courting with Beryl Butler and it is very close to the village of Priddy that he knew so well.

'TOBRUK'

After El Alamein, the most famous name in the battle for North Africa was without doubt Tobruk – a small port in Cyrenaica, the eastern province of Italian-occupied Libya. It had heroically withstood a siege of 240 days from 11 April to 27 November 1941. It was harassed by artillery, tanks and Stukas on a daily basis and was only kept re-supplied by ships of the Royal Navy operating out of Alexandria. Many ships were sunk either in harbour or on their way there. The harbour was littered with the masts of sunken vessels still protruding out of the water. The

Germans and Italians did in the end capture the port on 21 June 1942 after the hard-fought battles of Bir Hakeim and Gazala. Tobruk was recaptured from them ten days after El Alamein on 13 November 1942. John Jarmain and his anti-tank unit entered it soon afterwards.

In it he saw echoes of Italy and Troy, fought over ceaselessly for years on end. 'Its little harbour holds a hundred ships/ Which brave with cargoes came,/ Whose broken leaning masts like crazy posts/ Jut from the tranquil surface of the bay'. It is a shattered town populated only by 'alien ghosts.'

As always, Jarmain mulled this poem over in his mind and he finished it a month later whilst he was at Mersa Brega in mid-December 1942. The Desert War was moving very fast and so it was only when the Germans took up a defensive position that there was a chance to catch one's breath and let the supply lines sort themselves out, stockpiling ammunition for the next battle.

'NEW YEAR 1943'

This poem was written not far from Mersa Brega, at El Agheila. There were some horrendous casualties with booby traps and minefields here.

Added to this there had been a good deal of anxiety amongst the troops about their Christmas dinner, which had reportedly been sunk in Benghazi harbour. The rations only appeared at seven o'clock in the evening of Christmas Eve, so it was a close shave. The highland pipers no doubt wet their whistles as they had a supper of soup, turkey and pork, plum pudding and trimmings. Each man got 100 cigarettes and a bottle of beer. This was followed the next day by heavy rain and the salt marshes filled up nicely, which would have appealed to John Jarmain. On 29

December there was a disaster in the 2nd Seaforths, one of the three infantry battalions that John Jarmain's anti-tank battery was attached to. Three men had entered a minefield on patrol. They had all been wounded. In the subsequent 'rescue', ten men – including several officers – were killed, and another ten men were wounded.

The German 'S' mines that jumped in the air were very deadly indeed. It was one of these mines which wounded Keith Douglas in nearby Wadi Zem Zem.

THE BAND OF 51ST HIGHLAND DIVISION PLAYS IN
THE MAIN SQUARE IN TRIPOLI DURING A REVIEW BY
GENERAL MONTGOMERY, 28 JANUARY 1943.
TWO HUMBER MK II ARMOURED CARS CAN BE SEEN
IN THE FOREGROUND
© IMPERIAL WAR MUSEUMS (E 21969).

On New Year's Eve, the massed pipe bands of 152 Brigade, which comprised 2nd Seaforths, 5 Seaforths and the 5th Cameron Highlanders, beat the retreat at Divisional Headquarters. John Jarmain of course mentions none of this but looks up at the carpet of stars with 'The muffled sound of the sea and no sound else'. He is deep in a contemplative silence and links 'the quiet stars and the cold pale sand'. Like many soldiers, he is also contemplating the future and wondering what 1943 will bring. If it is anything like El Alamein and the minefields of Mersa Brega and El Agheila, they will be lucky to survive.

'LEPTIS MAGNA'

They arrive, tired but elated, at the ruins of Leptis Magna near Homs in the middle of the night with the moonlight shining on the marble columns. To quote from his letter of 22 January 1943, Jarmain is overwhelmed by its beauty, coming as he has done from many months in the desert:

"But the place itself I can never describe. I can only say that hitherto I have thought only Greece was great, I have thought Rome and her works prosaic and dull, and now suddenly I have seen her grandeur. Coming from the empty desert it was unspeakably amazing; and add that we arrived beside this ruined city at 12.30 a.m., and that as soon as jobs were done I went into it, and walked there from 1 a.m. to 2 a.m. in the white cold brilliance of a clear full moon, bigger and brighter here in Africa than your moons at home. The silence, the white moon-light, the smooth tall marble columns – I shall not quickly forget that hour. That, of course, is the real poem, beyond me to write."

His poem is ostensibly about having his hair cut, but

he reflects on the antiquity, the sense of history, the Italian archaeologists uncovering the city that their forefathers had built, and the act of the ant carrying off 'shreds of my hair, the buried city… / They are all disconnected, irrelevant one to another, / Incongruous. So I found them; so I have set them down.'

Jarmain is emphasising his own disconnectedness at being at Leptis Magna as part of a conquering army, no different to the Romans and Carthaginians slogging it out two thousand years earlier.

It was only 80 miles to Tripoli. They had already passed through 'Marble Arch' on the way out of Cyrenaica at the point they entered Tripolitania. Within a few days they were in Tripoli itself. Churchill flew out to see them and the pipe bands marched once more amongst the palm trees.

'PRISONERS OF WAR'

Although written in Sicily, this poem may well refer to the long streams of prisoners taken in North Africa. John Jarmain had a photograph album and in it is the iconic picture taken of prisoners after El Alamein. It matters little whether they be Germans or Italians. He is feeling some sort of empathy with them, possibly even sympathy: 'Like shabby ghosts down dried-up river beds / The tired procession slowly leaves the field'.

The image evokes that of a cricket team that has just been roundly defeated. But here the stakes are much, much higher. The prisoners are destined for some kind of limbo or half world. 'They file away, these who have done their last,/ To that grey safety where the days are sealed,/ Where no word enters, and the urgent past/ Is relieved day by day against the clock.' It is as if they are hovering above the asphodel meadows. Death has passed them by, and so has fear. They are in a stunned half life where they are condemned to safety for an indefinite period. 'They are quit of killing and sudden mutilation;/ They no longer cower at the sound of a shell in the air,/ They are safe.' And: 'They will return – old, worn maybe, but sure – /And gather their bits of broken lives to mend.'

This poem was written in Sicily after the thirty-nine day campaign which saw them landed near Cape Passero. There was some bitter fighting in the hills at Vizzini and Francoforte where 300 well-armed and expertly trained German paratroopers held up a brigade for a few days. Then there was Ramacca and the bitter fighting around Gerbini and in the Sferro hills to the west of Catania. John Jarmain was now commanding his own battery, 193 Battery, but was still part of the 51st Highland Division. After the war was over in Sicily, they had three months' relative peace and quiet where they had time to write letters and reflect upon the war.

Somehow the poetic spirit left John Jarmain for a while. To be sure, he wrote letters home and partied and listened to Chopin and Gracie Fields.

He visited Taormina and Messina and climbed Mount Etna; but the rigours of command somehow drained him of time and energy. It may be that the war was taking its toll in other ways; or maybe the party spirit in Sicily was just too good to be missed. He became very friendly with a Sicilian lady called Bianca Scafidi, the daughter of an old general. The Scafidis had a villa and they talked for hours and hours about literature and music. Bianca too was very fond of Jean Giono and d'Annunzio.

'THE INNOCENT SHALL SUFFER'

In November John Jarmain's battery sailed back to England and had some well-deserved leave. It was wet and wintry and they were stationed in the woods at Penn near Amersham. Training for D Day was now top of the list, including learning how to cross rivers without getting too wet or stalling vehicles, as well as amphibious landings. Live firing took place at Foulness, Harlech and Lulworth. It must have been very drab after North Africa and Sicily. There are only a few poems from this period.

This one is uncharacteristically long and labours the point that it is the innocent who usually suffer in an air raid. It draws the comparison between the young pilots and the civilians far below and how 'Like a gold rose the beaten cities burn' and how one young man 'saw the white heat at the flower's heart glow,/ And feathery rings of flaking petals spread'. Jarmain describes the pilot's girlfriend and then explores the dilemma facing women during war when her German counterpart 'Is in her sleep impersonally destroyed/ Whose room has walls of flame.' Jarmain raises the question of guilt and innocence and how it should be shared out: 'Guilty and innocent both is every one'. And all this before the great raids of early 1945.

In Cambridgeshire, Essex, Suffolk and Norfolk there were many RAF airfields; and stationed there were the bomber crews who went out on missions over Germany every night. Many did not return. Jarmain wrote this poem whilst staying at Dullingham near Newmarket. And he would certainly have met many young RAF bomber pilots in the nearby towns and pubs and talked to them about their raids. They even used the famous Newmarket racecourse as an aerodrome.

'FAILURE'

The failure is perhaps the personal failure to resolve the tenets of war with those of peace, the same dilemma highlighted in 'The Innocent Shall Suffer'. Maybe it is the anti-climax of coming home and having tasted victory in Egypt, Libya, Tunisia and Sicily; the 51st Highland Division felt that they had won their war, and won it in style.

Yet when they returned to Britain, the bleak, dark days of war were still around them and they knew full well that this next campaign would be very costly indeed. In February 1944 Jarmain is based in Foulness, a bleak spot at the best of times. As his letter of 7 February reveals:

'My room is far too cold for sitting up and writing you a real letter, but I want you to have something so that you do not feel forgotten.

Despite all the books I brought with me, I have not so far read a line, and this is the end of the second evening. However, I hope that that state of affairs will not last, and also that some sort of fuel will be procurable to give me a fire in my room. Coal seems very scarce here, at least for the army.'

John Jarmain is not in good sprits and he is also cold; and birdwatching is a real disappointment: 'Nor have I seen any birds, beyond a glimpse of a ring plover in flight as I drove by a dyke.' A single ring plover, to balance out the one he saw at El Alamein back in October 1942.

'BEGINNINGS'

This was originally in the section Peace-Time Poems but is very clearly a war time poem. As mentioned earlier, 'Beginnings' is really 'Endings' and in some ways echoes T.S. Eliot's 'East Coker' which was first published in 1940 and would have been well known to Jarmain: 'In my end is my beginning.' This could in a sense still apply to Jarmain himself, for in the poem there are echoes of his own creation; 'shamefaced lovely lust of his conceiving' is contrasted with the cause of his destruction: 'the smooth bright shapely shell/ And the great gun lifted gleaming in the air,/ Perfect with all the skill of men's contriving.'

Creation and destruction: two sides of the same coin. Beauty and perfection in death as in life.

'SILENCES'

This follows on from 'Beginnings' even though it was written in 1939. It describes the act of making love: 'bright as pain/ Was my desire. This hot astonishment/ With flush of flame burns up our quietness' which eventually 'Draws close the curtains of the silences.' A coming home, to a home which he still has in his mind from those rural pre-war days in Somerset.

'BARN OWL'

In a sense this closes the poems. It is the flight of the barn owl at dusk and has within it the image of old age when 'you and I will stand there together in the doorway,/ Saying to each other, "Look, the old owl's there."' Jarmain wrote this in August 1939, two months after he wrote 'Thinking of War'; so the cycle is complete. Even though his writing career was stopped short by a mortar bomb in St Honorine la Chardonnerette, there is a continuity in his writing that we can all pick up and read. It is his version of the magic realism of Jean Giono. Coincidentally, Honorine is a woman's name that crops up in *Que Ma Joie Remeure*. St Honorine of the Goldfinch...

Despite his death we can all learn from Jarmain how best to record war, at a slight angle and in a very human way, and it is not just through the shell's trajectory.

TROOPS COME ASHORE ON SWORD BEACH,
NORMANDY, 7 JUNE 1944 (D+1).
JOHN JARMAIN AND HIS BATTERY LANDED HERE
AND WERE SOON EMBROILED IN BITTER FIGHTING
IN THE VILLAGES AND ORCHARDS EAST OF CAEN
©IMPERIAL WAR MUSEUMS (A 24012)

'THOUGHTS FROM RANVILLE'

I am using a pencil because
I feel idle and prefer the smooth-sliding motion of it,
Although my pen is filled and in my pocket.

It is eleven in the evening, late twilight,
And raining spasmodically,
I am sitting by a hurricane lamp with Kaestlin

In an enormous doova
(two beds, two tables and room to stand up)
which was dug before we came here by some of our
paratroops.

It is very quiet save for the sound of the rain,
And when I have written this
I shall go to bed.

Now the quiet is disturbed
By the spitfires' evening patrol,
Passing overhead ensuring our peace.

They are out from dawn to dusk,
19 hours out of the 24, and only in dark
The enemy dares slip a few lonely raiders over the line.

The newspapers, which we receive
Only four days late, or less,
Have given sweet stories of flowers

And wine in French villages,
But so far I have seen none of it —
Only torn walls, burnt rafters,

Upturned trees and tangled telephone wires
Among the dust and mortar
And streets of ruined villages;

Little quiet country villages they were,
With church and calvary and estaminet,
Untenanted now.

Will these French, I wonder,
Be far-seeing enough
To forgive all this that we have brought,

And remember only that we came to set free, to save?
It will not be easy for them,
Returning after the destructive wave

Has passed over their homes,
And finding only wreckage, their cattle dead or strayed,
Their possessions destroyed or vanished away.

Some, the very young,
Show us in their faces that they are glad;
The rest, as one sees them returning

With handcarts and bicycles
To discover whether their houses stand or no,
Show faces unreadable, almost resigned.

How much I hope that soon the battle will move faster
And without halt, for in this way
The country is spared much of the damage.

WRITTEN IN THE LATE EVENING
25TH JUNE 1944. RANVILLE

John Jarmain was killed before dawn by mortar fire in the next village of St Honorine la Chardonnorette, less than six hours after writing this very letter. He is buried in the 6th Airborne cemetery in Ranville. A local French woman, Madame Lacroix tended his grave for many years. This was arranged by John Kaestlin.

REVIEWS OF WAR POEMS BY JOHN JARMAIN 1945-46

Jarmain speaks with steady certainty and related intensity.
Always lonely, he feels more isolated because of his deep
humanity and an unconscious responsibility for the
inhumanity that he cannot control.... He will be of
considerable stature in the final estimate of his war-poetry.

ALEC M. HARDIE TLS, 5TH JAN 1946

Jarmain was by nature a lover of silence...

ILLUSTRATED LONDON NEWS, 5TH JAN 1946

This slim volume will be appreciated by many.

NATIONAL NEWSAGENT

Sensitive as he evidently was to the horrors of war, he managed
in his poems to achieve an extraordinary tranquillity. His best
work, *Leptis Magna* has an affinity with that of Edward Thomas.

E.E. DUNCAN JONES - BIRMINGHAM POST, 5TH FEB 1946

Some of the earlier poems show the influence of Rupert
Brooke, but he out grew that and in writing of the desert or
of home struck a manly note of his own.

MANCHESTER GUARDIAN, 25TH JAN 1946

Obviously a man of well-trained intellectual force and character.

RICHARD CHURCH - JOHN O'LONDON'S WEEKLY
14TH DEC 1945

An ordered and balanced mind faced with war. Acceptance
rather than conflict is the mood from which these verses spring.

THE LISTENER, 10TH JAN 1946

Among the poets lost to us by the war, John Jarmain must
take a considerable place. A real loss.

VITA SACKVILLE-WEST - OBSERVER, JAN 13TH 1946

BRIEF BIOGRAPHIES

WILLIAM JOHN FLETCHER JARMAIN
1911-1944

Born in Hatch End, Pinner, Middlesex. Son of a chartered
surveyor. Educated at Shrewsbury School and Queens'
College Cambridge where he read Mathematics. Blue for
gymnastics. Moved to Somerset. Lived in Pilton, West
Pennard and Street. Taught at Millfield School. Joined up in
1939. Commissioned in July 1940. Served throughout the
Second War as a gunnery officer with 61st A/T Regt Royal
Artillery attached to 51st Highland Division. Trained in
Scotland 1940–1942. Served in North Africa with 242
Battery, August 1942 – May 1943. Fought at El Alamein,
Mersa Brega, El Agheila, Homs, Sirte, Buerat, Tripoli,
Medenine, Mareth, Wadi Akarit, Enfidaville. Then promoted
major and commanded 193 Battery. Training in Algeria
before Sicily landings in July 1943. Fought at Vizzini,
Ramacca, Gerbini and Sferro Hills. Returned to UK in
November 1943. Training for D Day billeted Penn Woods
near Amersham. Landed on Sword Beach D+1 Saw
extensive action east of the Orne bridgehead mainly around
Ranville and Escoville. Killed before breakfast at St Honorine
la Chardonnerette by a very unsporting German mortar
bomb on 26 June 1944.

Buried in 6th Airborne cemetery Ranville. Published
work: a novel *Priddy Barrows*, Collins 1944. *Poems* Collins
1945. Literary Agent A.M. Heath. Married twice. Eve
Houghton 1934 – two children: Mark and Joanna. Divorced
1939 then married Beryl Butler 1940. Three children: Janet,
Neil and Diana. His poems also appear in *The Daily
Telegraph, Convoy Magazine* and in several important
anthologies of 2nd World War Poets published by the
Salamander Oasis Trust.

JOHN (JEAN) PAUL KAESTLIN 1913-1963

Born in Switzerland, son of a bank manager. Naturalised
British citizen June 1939. Lived in 15 Montpelier Row,
Twickenham – where Tennyson had once lived. Educated at
Clifton College and St John's College, Cambridge where he
read Modern Languages. Worked as an editor and freelance
journalist before the war. Fluent in French, Spanish and
German. In 1937 he was employed as a staff interpreter at
Stoneham refugee camp near Eastleigh where nearly 4,000
Basque children were brought across on a ship, the *Habana*,
to escape the horrors of Guernica and the Spanish civil war.
Kaestlin enlisted in 1939. Commissioned 1940. Served in
61st Anti-Tank Battery 51st Highland Division in North
Africa, Sicily and Normandy 1942–1944. Was John Jarmain's
second-in-command in 193 A/T Battery. In late 1944 he
then transferred to HQ 21 Army Group A (Wehrmacht)
Branch as a staff officer helping to disband the German Army.
Not an easy job. Then he transferred to the staff of DAAG
(Deputy Assistant Adjutant-General) and worked with the
War Crimes Group N-W Europe prior to the Nuremberg
Trials. For this work he was awarded an MBE. He later
worked in the MOD London in Intelligence and also
commanded several artillery batteries, notably the 132
(Bengal Rocket Troop) Battery which had started life in 1816
in India with camels. Kaestlin was fascinated by the history of
artillery and became an expert on Congreve Rockets. After
leaving the army in 1959 he was called to the bar – the
Middle Temple – but did not practise. Instead he chose to
work at the Rotunda Artillery Museum at Woolwich as an
under-secretary in the historical branch. Here in just three
years he completely reorganised and modernised all the
exhibitions. Sadly he died in 1963 aged only fifty.

JOSEPH JOLYON DEAN 1921-2010

Joe Dean was the son of Basil Dean, the actor, entrepreneur and founder of Ealing studios who ran ENSA – Entertainments National Service Association – during the war. His mother was Esther Van Gruisen. He was educated at Harrow and Merton College, Oxford where he read Classics. When war interrupted his studies he joined up and was posted to 61st A/T Regiment Royal Artillery and went though North Africa, from El Alamein to Sicily and then Normandy with the 51st Highland Division. He was badly wounded at the First battle of St Honorine resulting in a long scar across his chest. After recovering from his wound he eventually rejoined his regiment. After the war had ended he went back to Oxford and read Jurisprudence. In 1947 he was called to the Bar by the Middle Temple and then specialised in Privy Council work in Africa and the West Indies. In 1975 he became a circuit judge. He was controversial, outspoken and had a great love of vernacular architecture. He wrote sketches for the paper Truth and in 1953, he published a collection of libel cases called *Hatred, Ridicule and Contempt*. In 1970 he wrote a short history of Middle Temple Hall. Sadly his autobiography, *Prisoner on the Bench*, was never finished. He was a great believer in the countryside and founded the East Ashford Rural Trust which opposed large-scale development of housing in Kent and opposed the scar of the proposed Channel tunnel railway line. In 1962 he married Jenefer Mills and they had three children: Antigone, Tacita (the film maker) and Ptolemy (the architect).

A BRITISH SIX POUNDER ANTI TANK GUN CREW IN
ACTION IN THE DESERT
© IMPERIAL WAR MUSEUMS (E 15560)